René Descartes

Thomas Edison

Margot Fonteyn

Michael Jackson

Jomo Kenyatta

Charles Lindbergh

Elvis Presley

Paul Revere

Sacagawea

Cy Young

Babe Didrickson Zaharias

Shaka Zulu

Written by Sean Price
Illustrated by Tony Tallarico

Incorporated

ABOUT THIS BOOK
Note to Parents and Teachers

GETTING CHILDREN'S ATTENTION

The Kids' Fun-Filled Biographies is a reference book that is fun to read. It has been specially created to inspire, inform, and entertain young readers. The colorful illustrations and brief-but-detailed biographies of fascinating people will draw children into the world of learning—and keep them there!

HELPING THEM EXPLORE KEY LIVES

Often, a child who is reading a book or watching television will come across someone's name and wonder, "Who was that person?" or "Why is this person famous?" *The Kids' Fun-Filled Biographies* is designed to answer those questions at a level that young readers can understand and enjoy. As they read about people who have made their mark on history, children will see how even ordinary people can sometimes accomplish extraordinary deeds. This is a book that children will turn to again and again as their knowledge of people and events grows.

THE ENTRIES IN THIS BOOK OF BIOGRAPHIES

The main achievements or major activities of more than 500 people are covered in *The Kids' Fun-Filled Biographies*. Each entry is accompanied by a colorful illustration of the person(s) in action. In the book's main section, entries appear alphabetically by surname. The index at the back of the book is arranged alphabetically by field of endeavor—artists, explorers, inventors, and so on—to help readers find the people who are of greatest interest to them.

BUILDING AN AT-HOME LIBRARY

An at-home library is best when it contains informational resources that are both educational and fun to read. *The Kids' Fun-Filled Biographies*, *The Kids' Fun-Filled Dictionary*, *The Kids' Fun-Filled Encyclopedia*, and *The Kids' Fun-Filled Question & Answer Book* do just that. They keep kids learning—and laughing!

Henry Louis (Hank) Aaron
Home-run King
1934-

On April 8, 1974, Atlanta Braves left fielder Hank Aaron made one of baseball's greatest hits. He whacked the ball into the left-center stands for his 715th career home run. That put him ahead of Babe Ruth as major-league baseball's all-time home-run king.

Aaron began his career in 1952 in the Negro American League. Two years later, he was playing for the Milwaukee (later Atlanta) Braves in the National League. In 23 seasons, Aaron hit 755 home runs and broke more batting records than any other player in history. He was elected to the Baseball Hall of Fame in 1982.

John Adams
Founding Father and 2nd U.S. President
1735-1826

Adams was one of the Founding Fathers of the U.S. Perhaps his greatest moment came in 1776, during the American Revolution. Many colonial leaders at that time still hoped to rejoin Great Britain. Adams pushed the Declaration of Independence through the Continental Congress instead.

After serving as George Washington's vice president, Adams became the second U.S. president in 1796. His blunt style created many enemies, however, and he lost the 1800 election to Thomas Jefferson. The election made Adams and Jefferson bitter enemies, but they later renewed their friendship. Both men died on July 4, 1826—the 50th anniversary of the signing of the Declaration of Independence. Adams was the father of the sixth U.S. president, John Quincy Adams.

Jane Addams
Social Reformer
1860-1935

Addams was one of the greatest social reformers in U.S. history. While in her 20s, Addams set up Hull House in Chicago. It was a neighborhood center where immigrants and poor people could get help with needs ranging from day care to college courses.

Addams put pressure on lawmakers to improve the plight of the poor. She was partly responsible for the first state child-labor laws and the creation of juvenile courts. She also fought to win voting rights for women, and championed research on the causes of crime and poverty. She was awarded the 1931 Nobel Peace Prize.

Konrad Adenauer
German Statesman
1876-1967

After World War II (1939-1945), Germany was shattered and divided. West Germany was occupied by the U.S. and its allies; East Germany was occupied by the Soviet Union. In 1949, West Germans elected Konrad Adenauer (AH-duh-NOW-ur) as their chancellor, or top leader. He helped build West Germany into a strong, peaceful country.

Before losing the war, Adolf Hitler's Nazis had imprisoned Adenauer for opposing them. When Adenauer became chancellor, he paid Jewish victims of the Holocaust and rebuilt West Germany's economy into the powerhouse of Europe. He served as chancellor until 1963. East and West Germany reunited in 1991, after the collapse of communism in Europe.

Aeschylus
Playwright
525-456 B.C.

Every television show and movie owes a debt to the Greek playwright Aeschylus (ESS-kuh-lus). Before he came along, the actors in a play consisted of one leader and a chorus in the background. Aeschylus came up with the idea of having two main actors who talked to each other. It was the birth of modern theater.

Aeschylus wrote about 90 plays, but only seven—such as *Agamemnon* and *Seven Against Thebes*—still survive. Despite the high praise he received as a writer, his proudest accomplishment was fighting in the Battle of Marathon in 490 B.C. That famous battle, which kept Persian invaders out of Greece, gives us the name for long-distance races today.

AESOP
STORYTELLER
UNKOWN-565 B.C.

According to ancient Greek tradition, Aesop *(EE-sop)* was the greatest fable teller of all time. Fables are brief stories that teach a lesson or make a point. Two of Aesop's most famous fables are "The Boy Who Cried Wolf" and "The Tortoise and the Hare."

Aesop was believed to be a slave who was disabled. Scholars today are unsure how many fables Aesop actually created. Some say that "Aesop" may have been several people. Whoever made them up, Aesop's fables were passed down by word of mouth for several hundred years before being written down around 300 B.C.

Louisa May Alcott
Author of *Little Women*
1832-1888

Alcott is author of the famous children's book *Little Women*. Her parents were friends with many great writers and thinkers, but Alcott's father handled money badly. She held several jobs at an early age—including seamstress and servant—in order to support her family.

Alcott turned to writing to get her family out of debt. In 1868, she published *Little Women*, a mostly autobiographical story about four sisters growing up in New England. Its success solved her financial problems and made her famous. She wrote several other books, though none achieved *Little Women*'s enduring fame.

Flower Fables
Hospital Sketches
Moods
Merry's Museum
Little Women
Little Men
Jo's Boys

Alexander the Great
Ancient Conqueror
356-323 B.C.

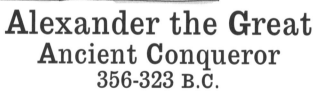

HE'S GREAT!

A true military genius, Alexander built an empire stretching from the Mediterranean Sea to India. His father, Philip, was the king of Macedonia (in what is now northern Greece). Philip had conquered all of Greece by the time he was killed. At age 20, Alexander took over as king and conquered the huge Persian empire.

As Alexander's power grew, he became arrogant and paranoid. He killed several friends he believed were plotting against him. Alexander died mysteriously at age 32, and his empire quickly broke apart. However, his conquests spread Greek learning and culture throughout Asia and North Africa.

Muhammad Ali
Boxing Champion
1942–

Ali is one of the most sensational figures in professional boxing. In 1978, he became the first heavyweight contender to win the title three times. Ali liked to call himself "the Greatest" and described his boxing style as "float like a butterfly, sting like a bee."

Born Cassius Marcellus Clay, he changed his name to Muhammad Ali when he became a Muslim in 1964. Ali was stripped of his championship in 1967 when he was convicted for refusing, on religious grounds, to join the U.S. Army to fight in the war in Vietnam. His conviction was later overturned by the U.S. Supreme Court.

Roald Amundsen
Polar Explorer
1872-1928

Roald Amundsen *(ROH-ald AHM-un-sun)* was a Norwegian explorer who helped discover the Antarctic South Pole in 1911. Amundsen and his team raced against a British expedition led by Robert F. Scott. Amundsen's group was well-prepared and beat Scott's by five weeks. Scott's team, which was poorly prepared, met a tragic end: All its members died of cold and hunger.

Amundsen spent most of his life exploring the Arctic. In 1926, he became one of the first people to fly over the North Pole. In 1928, Amundsen and several others died there while searching for a fellow explorer who had become lost.

Hans Christian Andersen
Storyteller
1805-1875

Few children grow up without hearing the fairy tales of Hans Christian Andersen. There are 156 of them, including "The Ugly Duckling" and "The Emperor's New Clothes." Andersen also wrote books and plays, but they are not as well-remembered.

Andersen grew up poor. His father was a shoemaker who died when Andersen was 11. Andersen struggled for many years as an actor before finally turning to writing. His fairy tales first became popular in the 1840s. They appeal to children because of their simplicity, but they also carry deeper messages intended for adults.

11

Marian Anderson
Singing Star
1902-1993

In 1939, concert singer Marian Anderson was barred from performing at Constitution Hall in Washington, D.C., because she was black. Outrage over the ban led to a concert for Anderson at the Lincoln Memorial before 75,000 people. One of the most famous concerts in U.S. history, it was a symbolic blow against racism.

Anderson is best remembered for that landmark concert. However, her soaring contralto voice made her a popular entertainer in the 1930s. In 1955, she became the first African American soloist with New York's Metropolitan Opera.

Susan B. Anthony
Champion of Women's Rights
1820-1906

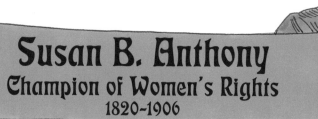

Susan B. Anthony was a major force in the drive to win voting rights for women in the U.S. She got her start in politics by fighting slavery and the abuse of alcoholic beverages. However, as a woman she was not allowed to speak at rallies. This pushed her to work for women's rights full time.

Anthony tried hard to publicize her movement. In 1872, she was arrested and fined for voting illegally in the presidential election. She died 14 years before the 19th Amendment to the Constitution gave women the right to vote. In 1979, the U.S. government issued dollar coins bearing her portrait.

Mark Antony
Statesman and General
83 B.C.-30 B.C.

Mark Antony is remembered as much for his passionate love affair with Cleopatra, Egypt's queen, as for his military skill. When Julius Caesar was assassinated in 44 B.C., Mark Antony seized power in Rome and defeated the assassins on the battlefield. In the turmoil that followed, Antony was forced to share power with Caesar's adopted son, Octavian (who would later be called Caesar Augustus) and a general named Lepidus.

Antony was given control over the eastern realm of Rome's empire, including Egypt. He soon fell in love with Cleopatra. Together, they plotted to control the whole Roman Empire. However, their armies were defeated.

Johnny Appleseed
Folk Hero
1774-1845

SOON WE CAN MAKE APPLESAUCE!

Yasir Arafat
Middle Eastern Leader
1929-

Yasir Arafat has been the leader of the Palestine Liberation Organization (PLO) since 1969. For many years, the PLO committed terrorist acts to regain land that they believed had been taken from them by the nation of Israel. In 1993, however, Arafat signed a peace agreement with Israel that allowed Palestinians to control some of their own territories.

Because of the 1993 agreement, Arafat was a co-winner of the 1994 Nobel Peace Prize. In January 1996, Arafat was elected the first president of the Palestinian Council governing the disputed lands—the West Bank and Gaza Strip.

Johnny Appleseed's real name was John Chapman. He reportedly planted apple trees throughout Ohio, Indiana, and Illinois as settlers moved westward. However, very little is actually known about Chapman. The first article about him appeared 26 years after his death.

According to legend, however, Johnny Appleseed gave away apple seeds and saplings to everyone he saw. He also used a tin pot for a hat, a coffee sack for a shirt, and did not wear shoes. Chapman reportedly never carried a gun and gave all his money to the poor. He also walked hundreds of miles to plant and tend apple trees.

Archimedes
Mathematician and Inventor
287-212 B.C.

Archimedes (AR-kuh-MEE-deez) was the greatest math wiz and inventor in the ancient world. Among other things, he advanced the use of levers and pulleys, which allowed people to move large objects. He boasted, "Give me a place to stand on and I will move the world."

Archimedes was a Greek who lived in Syracuse, Sicily. When Syracuse was attacked by the Romans, he invented giant cranes that could flip and destroy ships. They helped hold off the Romans' invasion for three years. When the city finally fell, tradition says, a Roman soldier killed Archimedes while he worked on a geometry problem.

Aristotle
Philosopher and Scientist
384-322 B.C.

It is hard to find an area of science, mathematics, or philosophy that the Greek genius Aristotle (*AR-uh-STOT-ul*) did not pioneer. He studied zoology and physics, founded the use of logic and comparative anatomy, and made the first scientific study of politics and law.

A student of Plato, another famous philosopher, Aristotle became the personal tutor to Alexander the Great. During the Middle Ages in Europe, especially the 1100s and 1200s, many people believed that Aristotle had summed up all knowledge. Since then, many of his ideas have been proven wrong. However, his logical approach to research still influences science today.

Louis Armstrong
Jazz Trumpeter
1901-1971

Growing up poor in the slums of New Orleans, Louis Armstrong sang on street corners for tips. At 14, he learned to play trumpet and began by playing in nightclubs. In the 1920s, jazz music was still considered a new musical form, and Armstrong's inventive playing, not to mention his warm personality, brought the music to a wider audience.

Armstrong, who was nicknamed "Satchmo," was known for his gravelly singing voice and skillful trumpet playing. His hit songs included "Hello, Dolly" and "What a Wonderful World." Armstrong, who spoke out strongly against racism, also served as a goodwill ambassador for the U.S.

Neil Armstrong
First Person on the Moon
1930-

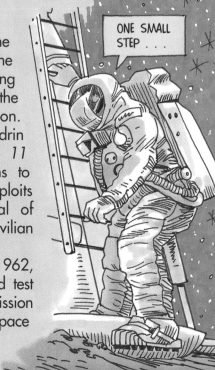

ONE SMALL STEP . . .

"That's one small step for [a] man, one giant leap for mankind." Those were the words that U.S. astronaut Neil Armstrong used on July 20, 1969, as he became the first person to walk on the moon. Armstrong and Edwin E. ("Buzz") Aldrin Jr., his crew mate from the *Apollo 11* spacecraft, became the first humans to explore the moon. Armstrong's exploits earned him the Presidential Medal of Freedom—the highest award a U.S. civilian can receive.

Armstrong became an astronaut in 1962, after serving as a Navy jet flyer and test pilot. In 1986, he served on the commission that investigated the explosion of the space shuttle *Challenger*.

Arthur Ashe
Tennis Star
1943-1993

In 1968, Arthur Ashe became the first black man to win the U.S. men's national singles championship and, in 1975, the first black man to win the Wimbledon singles championship. After retiring from tennis in 1980, he wrote a three-volume history of African American athletes called *A Hard Road to Glory*.

Ashe was known for his gentlemanly behavior on the court and his outspoken stance against racism. In 1983, he received a transfusion of blood tainted with the AIDS virus. He became a campaigner for the rights of AIDS patients. Three months before he died, Ashe addressed the United Nations (UN) on the importance of boosting AIDS research.

Isaac Asimov
Science-fiction Writer
1920-1992

Isaac Asimov *(AZ-uh-mahv)* was one of the top science-fiction writers of the 20th century. He was a brilliant man who also wrote knowledgeably about science, religion, history, and other topics. He aimed to make complicated subjects easy enough for ordinary readers to understand.

Asimov began writing stories when he was 11 years old. As an adult, he wrote nearly every day, churning out more than 500 books in his lifetime. He was a strong supporter of science and reason, and was well-known for opposing all beliefs based on superstition. Among his most famous books are the *Foundation* series; *I, Robot*; and *The Martian Way and Other Stories*.

John Jacob Astor
Fur Trader and Entrepreneur
1763-1848

John Jacob Astor was the Bill Gates of his day, amassing the greatest fortune in early U.S. history. Astor immigrated to the U.S. from Germany when he was 21. Though nearly penniless at the time, he opened a small fur shop in Baltimore. By the early 1800s, his company had a monopoly on the fur trade and Astor became wealthy.

Astor bought up land near New York City, betting that the city would grow. He was right. When he died, his estate was worth $20 million—an amount that would be worth close to $80 billion today.

Kemal Atatürk
Leader of Turkey
1881-1938

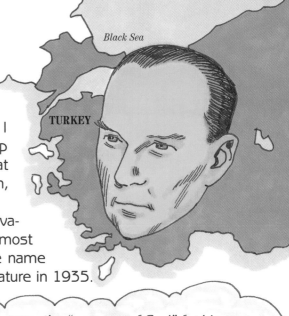

Black Sea

TURKEY

Kemal Atatürk (kuh-MAHL AT-uh-TURK) was a World War I hero who overthrew the corrupt Ottoman dynasty and set up the modern republic of Turkey. He launched radical reforms that modernized the country, including voting rights for women, improved education, and a European-style system of laws.

Many of Atatürk's reforms clashed with the views of conservative Muslims. His legacy is still debated among today's Turks, most of whom are Muslim. Born Mustafa Kemal, he was given the name Atatürk—which means "father of the Turks—by Turkey's legislature in 1935.

ATTILA
ANCIENT CONQUEROR
A.D. 406?-453

I'M LATE FOR LUNCH!

Attila was known as the "scourge of God" for his many attacks on the crumbling Roman Empire during the A.D. 400s. Attila had his own massive empire, which stretched from Germany to the Caspian Sea. He created it by uniting the Huns, who were based in modern-day Hungary, and invading neighboring lands.

Attila's biggest threat to the Roman Empire came in 451, when he invaded an area that now belongs to France. His attack was stopped by the Romans in a bloody battle. Attila died two years later and his empire quickly collapsed. The Roman Empire fell apart in 476.

John James Audubon
Naturalist and Artist
1785-1851

QUICK— PAINT ME!

John James Audubon was the first great wildlife artist in the U.S. As a young man, he failed several times as a businessman. At one point in 1819, he was jailed for debts that he could not pay. After that, his wife worked to support him while he painted a collection of detailed artwork of North American birds.

In 1826, his collection of bird paintings was published. It became a smashing success, earning him fame and fortune. After that, Audubon continued painting other North American animals while studying them and writing about their behavior.

Augustus
Roman Emperor
63 B.C.-A.D. 14

THE MONTH OF AUGUST IS NAMED AFTER ME.

Augustus became the first and greatest of the Roman emperors. He ruled Rome during its golden age, when Roman literature and architecture reached new heights and Rome's military power was unmatched. Augustus was a dictator, but he ruled justly for the most part.

Born with the name Octavian, he became the adopted son of Julius Caesar. When Caesar was assassinated in 44 B.C., Octavian fought a long civil war with Mark Antony for control of Rome. After Octavian won, Rome's Senate gave him the name Augustus, which means "sacred." The month of August gets its name from him.

Jane Austen
Novelist
1775-1817

WHAT SHALL I WRITE TODAY?

One of the first great female writers, Jane Austen specialized in turning ordinary situations into fascinating stories. She came from a well-off family, and all six of her novels are populated by characters from England's wealthy classes. The three most famous of her books are *Pride and Prejudice*, *Sense and Sensibility*, and *Emma*.

Austen began writing as a young girl, but did not publish her first book until after she was 30. All her novels revolve around young women facing the prospect of marriage. There is very little action. Instead, the stories focus on internal conflicts and everyday problems.

Charles Babbage
Inventor of the First Computer
1791-1871

I WONDER: WILL COMPUTERS EVER BE POPULAR?

An English inventor and mathematician, Babbage is often called the "father of computing." He designed two calculating machines that were forerunners of the modern computer. Only one was built; the British government stopped funding the second. Babbage fought to get the project going again, but other experts considered his plans "worthless." Next, Babbage designed an "analytical engine"—a machine that could perform any mathematical operation using instructions fed into it with punched cards. Saddened by his earlier defeat, he never sought funding for the third machine.

This machine was forgotten until Babbage's notebooks were rediscovered in 1937. When scientists built it in 1991, they found that Babbage's invention could accurately calculate numbers 31 digits long! It worked in a way remarkably similar to modern-day computers.

Johann Sebastian Bach
Composer
1685-1750

THIS IS FROM MY BRANDENBURG CONCERTO.

J. S. Bach was one of the most important musicians of the 1700s. During his lifetime, the German-born Bach was an organist who played for churches and royalty. In his day, the music he composed was considered old-fashioned, and his work was ignored after his death. In the 1820s, however, his compositions were rediscovered, studied, and played—and Bach was finally hailed as one of the greatest composers of the Western world. Many Bach works, such as the *Brandenburg Concertos* and "Jesu, Joy of Man's Desiring," are instantly familiar to many people today. Bach was a master of musical form called a fugue *(fyoog)*, in which different instruments repeat the same melody over and over again. Four of Bach's 20 children became famous musicians in their own right.

Francis Bacon
Statesman and Philosopher
1561-1626

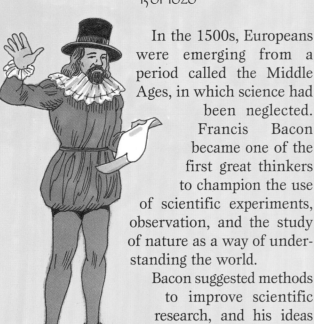

In the 1500s, Europeans were emerging from a period called the Middle Ages, in which science had been neglected. Francis Bacon became one of the first great thinkers to champion the use of scientific experiments, observation, and the study of nature as a way of understanding the world.

Bacon suggested methods to improve scientific research, and his ideas were quickly adopted. A powerful politician, he used his influence to promote science and philosophy. In 1621, however, Bacon was disgraced for taking a bribe. He spent the rest of his life in seclusion.

James Baldwin
Noted Author
1924-1987

THIS WAS MY FIRST NOVEL.

Go Tell It on the Mountain (1953)

A novelist, playwright, and essayist, James Baldwin became famous during the 1950s and 1960s for his attacks on racial injustice in the U.S. His works stress his belief that, regardless of race or culture, we are all human beings and should be treated as such. Two of his most popular books are *Nobody Knows My Name* and *The Fire Next Time*.

Baldwin grew up in Harlem in New York City, the oldest of nine children. At age 14, he became a minister, but he soon left the ministry to write full-time. In 1948, he won a literary prize that awarded him money that he used to travel to France. He spent much of his adult life there.

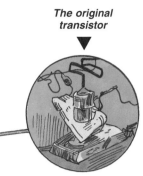

The original transistor ▼

John Bardeen
1908-1991

Walter H. Brattain
1902-1987

&

William Shockley
1910-1989

Inventors of the Transistor

Imagine a world without personal computers or portable CD players. That is what it would be like if Bardeen, Brattain, and Shockley had not invented the transistor in 1947. Transistors are tiny devices that control the flow of electric current. Thousands of them can fit in the space of one postage stamp! That miniature size allows engineers to make televisions, radios, and other electronic equipment that is smaller, cheaper, and better.

The three scientists won the 1956 Nobel Prize for physics for their work. Bardeen became the first man to win the Nobel Prize twice in the same field: He also shared the 1972 Nobel Prize for physics.

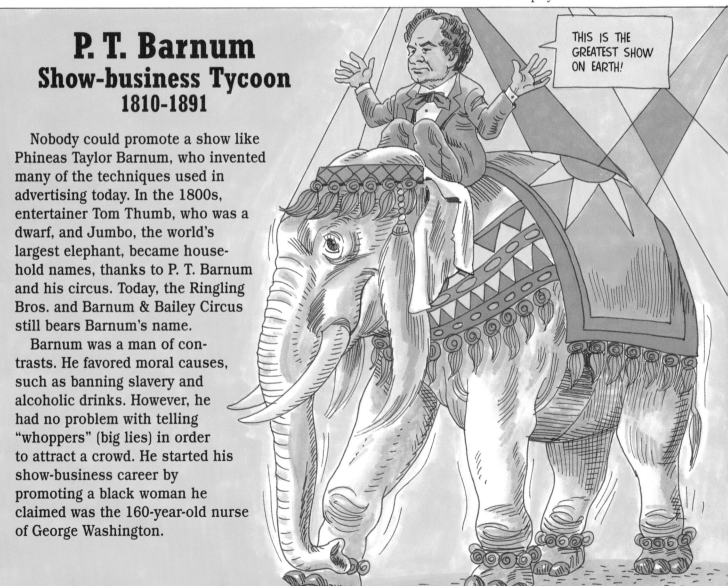

P. T. Barnum
Show-business Tycoon
1810-1891

Nobody could promote a show like Phineas Taylor Barnum, who invented many of the techniques used in advertising today. In the 1800s, entertainer Tom Thumb, who was a dwarf, and Jumbo, the world's largest elephant, became household names, thanks to P. T. Barnum and his circus. Today, the Ringling Bros. and Barnum & Bailey Circus still bears Barnum's name.

Barnum was a man of contrasts. He favored moral causes, such as banning slavery and alcoholic drinks. However, he had no problem with telling "whoppers" (big lies) in order to attract a crowd. He started his show-business career by promoting a black woman he claimed was the 160-year-old nurse of George Washington.

19

Clara Barton
Founder of the American Red Cross
1821–1912

When the U.S. Civil War broke out in 1861, Clara Barton left her job to feed and nurse Union soldiers. Her bravery and compassion earned her the nickname "Angel of the Battlefield." After the war, she led a campaign to search for missing soldiers. Without her efforts, thousands of dead men would have been listed as missing in action.

After the war, she founded the American Red Cross, an organization that aided people caught in wars and natural disasters. Barton pushed the U.S. to sign the Geneva Convention of 1864, which helped to protect sick and wounded soldiers during wartime. She also championed women's right to vote, which was not achieved until 1920.

Mikhail Baryshnikov
Ballet Star
1948-

Mikhail Baryshnikov (buh-RISH-nih-kov) is one of the greatest ballet dancers of the 20th century. He was unmatched as a ballet star in the 1970s and 1980s, in part because he took daring risks that made his performances more exciting. He danced the major male roles in all of the famous ballets from the 1800s, as well as in many modern works.

Weary of the repression in his native Soviet Union, Baryshnikov defected to Canada in 1974. His good looks and acting talent made him popular in movies as well. In 1977, he earned an Academy Award nomination for his role in *The Turning Point*. He is currently the director of the White Oak Dance Project, a modern-dance company.

COUNT BASIE
JAZZ BAND LEADER
1904–1984

William "Count" Basie was a popular band leader during the jazz swing era of the 1930s and 1940s. Basie got his nickname early in his career as a disc jockey. He spent many hungry years as an up-and-coming musician, but by the late 1930s his band had won international fame.

In the 1950s, young people began turning away from the big-band sound and toward rock and roll. However, the Count Basie Orchestra continued to record and perform, remaining a strong influence in the world of jazz.

Ibn Battuta
World Traveler
1304-1368

A native of Morocco, Ibn Battuta (IB-un buh-TOO-tuh) has been called "the Marco Polo of Islam." At age 21, he began a series of travels that took him more than 75,000 miles and took 30 years to complete. He wandered throughout northern Africa and southern Asia, making it all the way to China.

Ibn Battuta traveled widely at a time when most people never left their hometowns. Travelers faced constant danger from disease, robbers, shipwrecks, and the weather. When he returned to Morocco in 1354, Ibn Battuta dictated a history of his adventures called the *Rihduläh*.

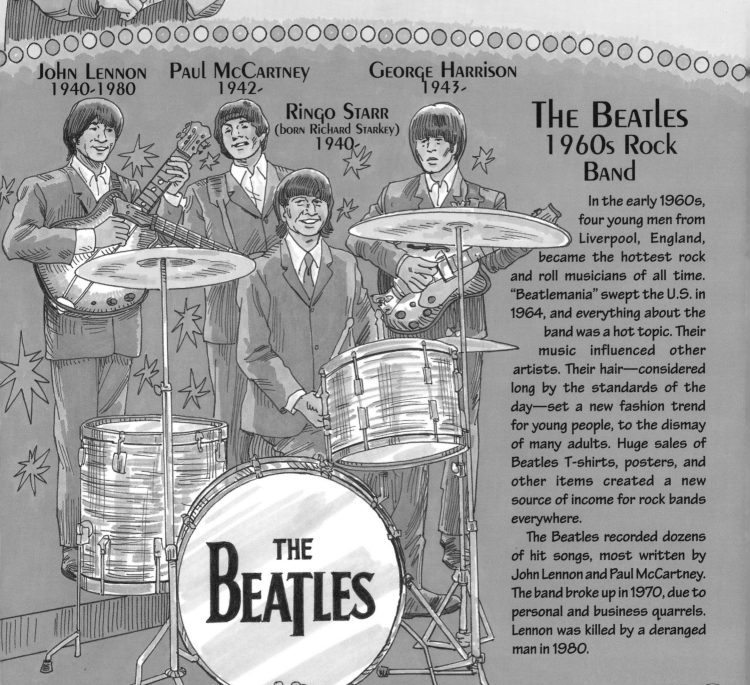

JOHN LENNON
1940-1980

PAUL McCARTNEY
1942-

GEORGE HARRISON
1943-

RINGO STARR
(BORN RICHARD STARKEY)
1940-

The Beatles
1960s Rock Band

In the early 1960s, four young men from Liverpool, England, became the hottest rock and roll musicians of all time. "Beatlemania" swept the U.S. in 1964, and everything about the band was a hot topic. Their music influenced other artists. Their hair—considered long by the standards of the day—set a new fashion trend for young people, to the dismay of many adults. Huge sales of Beatles T-shirts, posters, and other items created a new source of income for rock bands everywhere.

The Beatles recorded dozens of hit songs, most written by John Lennon and Paul McCartney. The band broke up in 1970, due to personal and business quarrels. Lennon was killed by a deranged man in 1980.

SAMUEL BECKETT
INFLUENTIAL POET, NOVELIST, AND PLAYWRIGHT
1906-1989

Samuel Beckett was one of the most influential writers of the 20th century. His plays, which had unusual plots and characters, changed what playwrights and audiences thought a play could be. He won the 1969 Nobel Prize for literature. In 1937, while still a struggling writer, he moved to Paris from his native Ireland. When World War II broke out two years later, France was overrun by Nazi Germany. Beckett became a member of the French Resistance, a group that opposed the Nazis. He once barely escaped capture by the Germans.

After the war, Beckett remained in France. His play *Waiting for Godot* made him world-famous in 1953. He later branched out into writing for radio and television. However, he was best-known for writing edgy, experimental plays—including *Endgame* and *Footfalls*—that changed the way theater was done.

Ludwig van Beethoven
Composer
1770-1827

DON'T FORGET TO PRACTICE!

After meeting Beethoven as a young man, the great composer Mozart said, "He will give the world something worth listening to." Mozart was right. Beethoven spent his life writing immortal classics, including his Fifth Symphony, Ninth Symphony, and the "Moonlight Sonata." Many of his works sparked controversy, because they broke long-held rules about music.

Beethoven came from a poor and unstable German family. His talent as a musician showed early on, and by age 18 he was the family's main breadwinner. Tragedy haunted Beethoven all his life. Around 1796, he began going deaf. Within a few years, he was unable to hear the beautiful music he still created.

Alexander Graham Bell
Inventor of the Telephone
1847-1922

IF I CALLED WATSON TODAY, I'D GET A BUSY SIGNAL.

In the mid-1800s, the telegraph—signals sent in the dots and dashes of Morse code—was the most high-tech form of communication. In 1874, Bell began trying to send human voices over electrical wires. During one experiment in 1876, he and his assistant, Thomas Watson, were in different rooms as they tried a new transmitter. Watson clearly heard Bell say, "Mr. Watson, come here. I want you." It was the first telephone call.

Bell became wealthy from his new invention. He devoted his life to several causes, including promoting science and helping the deaf. He also helped organize the National Geographic Society, which still publishes *National Geographic* magazine.

David Ben-Gurion
First Prime Minister of Israel
1886-1973

David Ben-Gurion was one of the driving forces behind the creation of the modern nation of Israel. Once it was established in 1948, Ben-Gurion led the country for most of its first 15 years. Those years were filled with tension and fighting between Israel and its Arab neighbors.

Ben-Gurion was born David Gruen in Russia. In 1906, he moved to the area that was then Palestine and took the name *Ben-Gurion*, which means "son of the young lion" in Hebrew. Ben-Gurion soon came a leader of the Zionists, a group working to create a Jewish homeland in Palestine.

Milton Berle
Comedian and TV Pioneer
1908-

For most Americans living in the early 1950s, Tuesday nights belonged to Milton Berle. He was the host of the *Texaco Star Theater* on NBC, a variety show that featured dancing and music as well as slapstick comedy by "Uncle Miltie" himself.

Berle's show first aired in 1948, when television was in its infancy. It quickly became one of the first hit shows, and it is credited with making TV more popular. Because of that, Berle—who was born with the last name Berlinger—is often called "Mr. Television."

Irving Berlin
Composer
1888-1989

Irving Berlin dominated the U.S. music world in the early 1900s. Another composer said, "Irving Berlin has no place in American music. He *is* American music." Berlin wrote dozens of popular songs, including "God Bless America" and "White Christmas." He also wrote music for plays and movies, including *The Jazz Singer* and *Annie Get Your Gun*.

Born Israel Beilin in Russia, Berlin changed his name when he immigrated to the U.S. in 1893. His father died when he was 13, so Berlin spent years in poverty, doing odd jobs. In 1911, he wrote his first hit song, "Alexander's Ragtime Band."

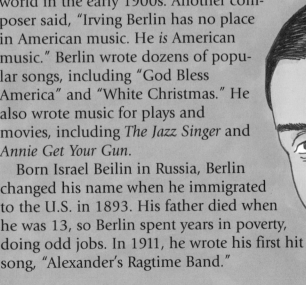

Leonard Bernstein was one of the top American conductors and composers in the late 1900s. He rose to fame in 1943, when he filled in for another pianist who had become ill. The concert was broadcast nationally on radio, and Bernstein did so well that he was instantly in demand.

Leonard Bernstein
Composer
1918-1990

Bernstein is probably best-known for the musicals he wrote, including *On the Town* and *West Side Story*. He had close ties to the New York Philharmonic orchestra, serving as its conductor on numerous occasions. He made a special effort to teach music to young people.

Mary McCleod Bethune
Noted Educator
1875-1955

A child of slaves, Mary McCleod Bethune grew up in South Carolina, picking cotton. As a young girl, she had to walk five miles to school each day. She pursued her studies, though, and in 1904 she set up her own school in Florida. Today, it is known as Bethune-Cookman College.

Bethune believed that education was the key to equal rights for black Americans. She was also a feminist who mobilized thousands of black female activists. In 1936, President Franklin D. Roosevelt named her director of the Division of Negro Affairs in the National Youth Administration. That made her the first African American woman to head a federal agency.

Billy the Kid
Western Outlaw
1859-1881

Almost everything about Billy the Kid is shrouded in mystery. The number of people he killed could be as low as five or as high as 21. No one knows for certain. It is clear, though, that he was a cattle thief, loner, and killer who spent his late teens and early twenties roaming the New Mexico territory.

Billy's real name also causes confusion. He was born Henry McCarty in New York City. However, he used several aliases, including William H. Bonney. Billy the Kid slipped through the fingers of law-enforcement officials many times before being gunned down by Sheriff Pat Garrett at Fort Sumner, New Mexico.

Otto von Bismarck
Leader of Germany
1815-1898

As chancellor (top leader) of Germany, Bismarck was the most powerful politician in Europe during the late 1800s. He took several loosely connected German states and molded them into a powerful empire. His ruthlessness earned him the name "the Iron Chancellor."

Bismarck said that political problems had to be settled with "blood and iron" rather than speeches. He was true to his word. Between 1864 and 1871, he helped launch three wars designed to unify Germany. He was also a clever politician who knew how to avoid a fight when it was not in Germany's best interest.

BLACK HAWK
SAUK AND FOX INDIAN WARRIOR
1767-1838

In the early 1800s, white settlers were forcing the Sauk and Fox Indians off their ancestral lands in Illinois. Most chiefs peaceably moved out of Illinois to west of the Mississippi River. However, Black Hawk refused to give up his land.

In 1832, he led 1,500 followers back across the Mississippi. During the Black Hawk War, his forces fought several brief battles in Illinois before being chased into Wisconsin. Deserted by his Indian allies, Black Hawk was defeated at the Battle of Bad Axe. After being imprisoned briefly, he wrote an autobiography that has become a classic.

YOU CAN GO BACK TO SCHOOL TOMORROW.

Elizabeth Blackwell
First Female Doctor in the U.S.
1821-1910

In 1847, the Geneva Medical College in Geneva, New York, created a storm of controversy when it allowed Blackwell—a woman—to study there. Two years later, when she graduated first in her class, Blackwell became the first woman in U.S. history to be awarded a medical degree.

At first, other doctors refused to work with Blackwell because of her gender. Gradually though, she earned their respect. In 1868, in New York, she opened the Women's Medical College. In 1869, she returned to England, where she was born, and spent the rest of her life fighting to help other women enter the medical profession.

Judy Blume
Novelist
1938-

Judy Blume is one of the most popular—and controversial—authors writing for pre-teens and teenagers. Her novels frequently deal with the problems of teenagers, including sexual issues. Because of that, there have been several efforts to ban Blume's books from local school and public libraries.

Blume's books especially appeal to young girls. Some of her most popular titles include *Are You There, God? It's Me, Margaret* and *Then Again, Maybe I Won't*. Her book *Tales of a Fourth-Grade Nothing* is one of the highest-selling trade paperback books for children.

Nellie Bly
Crusading Journalist
1867-1922

I CIRCLED THE GLOBE BETWEEN NOVEMBER 14, 1889, AND JANUARY 25, 1890, FOLLOWING THE PATH OF PHILEAS FOGG, HERO OF JULES VERNE'S NOVEL *AROUND THE WORLD IN 80 DAYS.* WHAT A TRIP!

Elizabeth Cochrane used the pen name Nellie Bly while she worked as a reporter in New York City. Bly took huge risks. She once had herself committed to a mental hospital to find out what conditions were like there. What she discovered was so horrible that her articles about it soon led to reforms.

Bly began her career at the age of 18, when she wrote a letter to a Pittsburgh newspaper in favor of women's rights. It was so good that the paper hired her. When Bly was working in New York, a rival newspaper called her the "best reporter in America."

Simón Bolívar
South American Liberator
1783-1830

Simón Bolívar *(see-MOAN buh-LEE-vahr)* is often called "the George Washington of South America." From 1819 to 1824, he led a series of brilliant military campaigns against Spanish forces in South America. Those victories ended Spanish colonial rule on the continent.

Bolívar hoped that the newly liberated countries would unite, but squabbling among various groups shattered that dream. Bolívar also wanted to set up freely elected governments. However, he soon became a dictator, and public opinion swung against him. He resigned in disgust and was preparing to leave South America when he died.

DANIEL BOONE
FRONTIERSMAN
1734-1820

Daniel Boone is the model of the daring, restless pioneer. He got his first rifle at age 12 and quickly became an expert marksman, hunter, and trapper. He loved living in the wild. Boone helped to blaze the Wilderness Road, a pathway that allowed thousands of settlers to move westward into Kentucky. Boone's adventures often led to fighting with Native Americans. He was captured four times by them, managing to escape each time. However, his deep respect for and knowledge of Native American ways helped to prevent bloodshed between settlers and Native Americans on many occasions.

MARGARET BOURKE-WHITE
PHOTOGRAPHER AND JOURNALIST
1906-1971

During the 1930s and 1940s, the photo magazine *Life* was a window on the world for most Americans. Margaret Bourke-White was one of *Life*'s greatest photographers, an unusual accomplishment for any woman at that time. She also became the first female war correspondent in World War II, and covered the war from several battlefronts.

Bourke-White helped create the photo essay—using a collection of photos to tell a story, instead of just one. In 1952, she was struck with Parkinson's disease, an ailment that slowly reduces muscle control. After that, she devoted most of her time to writing.

Omar Bradley
World War II General
1893-1981

Omar Bradley was one of the most popular and successful U.S. generals in World War II. He personally directed the invasion of France on D-Day in June 1944. He also commanded more than 1.3 million U.S. soldiers—called GIs—as they swept across France and into Nazi Germany.

Bradley became known as "the GI's general" because of his mild-mannered nature and genuine concern for ordinary soldiers. After the war, he served in a variety of high-level Army posts. Bradley became a five-star general—the highest rank in the U.S. Army—and remained on active duty for the rest of his life.

Mathew Brady
Civil War Photographer
1823-1896

MY WAGON IS MY DARKROOM.

Mathew Brady is known as the greatest photographer of the U.S. Civil War. But Brady, who was well-known for taking portrait photographs of famous Americans, took few of the war photos himself. Instead, he hired a team of 100 top-notch cameramen to visit the battlefields and army camps. Their photos carried his name.

Brady's photos make up the best visual record of the Civil War. After the war, however, few people bought his photos—most Americans wanted to forget about the fighting. Finally, the U.S. Congress purchased the whole lot for $25,000, all of which went to pay off Brady's debts. He died penniless.

Louis Braille
Invented Writing for the Blind
1809-1852

A   B   F   G   H

I   J   N   O   P

As a 15-year-old student, Louis Braille invented a code of raised dots on paper known today as Braille. The dots represent letters of the alphabet, allowing blind people to read by running their fingers over the paper.

Braille, who lived in France, went blind at age three due to a serious illness. He invented the Braille system because he wanted more books to read. The idea for the code came to him after he heard about military codes that allowed officers to read messages in the dark. Braille's system took several years to catch on, but today it is accepted worldwide.

Louis Brandeis
Supreme Court Justice
1856-1941

Lewis Brandeis was the first Jewish justice to sit on the U.S. Supreme Court. His razor-sharp intellect won him high grades at Harvard Law School. When he graduated at age 21, he became known as "the people's attorney" because he often took cases that challenged the power of big companies, such as railroads. He also took on poor clients and refused to charge them.

Some people disapproved of his activism. When President Woodrow Wilson nominated Brandeis to the high court in 1916, there was a bitter debate in the U.S. Senate, which had to approve or deny the nomination. However, Brandeis was confirmed. He served as a Supreme Court justice until 1939.

Bertolt Brecht
Playwright
1898-1956

Bertolt Brecht *(BUR-tawlt brehkt)* wrote plays more to influence people's opinions than entertain them. He was a reformer who believed that the capitalist economic system hurt the poor and made the rich greedy. Brecht also supported "epic theater," which often resulted in a very unemotional acting style.

Nevertheless, he produced several plays of great power. His biggest success came in 1928, with *The Threepenny Opera*. Brecht had to flee from Germany in 1933, when the Nazis came to power. He lived in the U.S. for several years. After World War II, however, he moved to East Germany.

The Brontë Sisters
Novelists

Anne Brontë
1820-1849

Emily Brontë
1818-1848

Charlotte Brontë
1816-1855

In 1847, three members of the Brontë family of Yorkshire, England, became famous novelists. Anne published *Agnes Grey*, Emily published *Wuthering Heights*, and Charlotte published *Jane Eyre*—all within a few months of each other.

Agnes Grey has faded in importance, but *Wuthering Heights* and *Jane Eyre* remain two of the most famous novels in the English language. Both are tragic love stories set on the windswept moors of Yorkshire.

Wuthering Heights, a story about two ill-fated lovers, was criticized at first for showing too much unrestrained passion. *Jane Eyre*, which was an instant success, is a largely autobiographical book about a governess (live-in teacher) who falls in love with her employer.

The Brontës were well-educated, but their family was poor and not socially connected. The sisters lived at the family home, even as adults.

Jim Brown
NFL Running Back
1936-

Jim Brown was one of the greatest running backs in National Football League (NFL) history. During his nine years with the Cleveland Browns, he led the league in rushing for eight seasons. Brown had the power to run over defensive players, but his speed and ability to slip through tackles usually made that unnecessary.

Brown surprised football fans in 1966 by retiring at the age of 30. He had decided to become a movie actor. His career rushing record of 12,312 yards stood for nearly two decades before being broken in 1984. Brown was elected to the Pro Football Hall of Fame in 1971.

John Brown
Radical Abolitionist
1800-1859

In 1859, John Brown and several followers raided the U.S. arsenal (a place where arms and ammunition are stored) at Harper's Ferry, Virginia. They hoped to start a slave rebellion, but the plan backfired. Brown was tried, found guilty, and hanged. His followers were caught or killed. Historians consider Brown's raid to be one of the sparks that set off the U.S. Civil War. It greatly increased mistrust between Southerners, who allowed slavery, and Northerners, who did not.

Years before the raid, Brown had massacred proslavery settlers in Kansas. Although many Americans disapproved of Brown's violent tactics in Kansas and at Harper's Ferry, his devotion to the antislavery cause earned him admirers in the North.

William Jennings Bryan
Statesman
1860-1925

William Jennings Bryan was a politician and fiery public speaker who ran for president, as a Democrat, three times between 1896 and 1908. He was defeated each time. He was well-known for being able to electrify crowds with the power of his words.

Bryan, a fundamentalist Christian, played a leading role in the 1925 trial of John Scopes. Scopes was a schoolteacher accused of teaching that humans evolved from apes, which violated a Tennessee state law. Bryan assisted the prosecution, while Clarence Darrow, a famous lawyer, defended Scopes. Bryan won the trial, but popular opinion swung against him and antievolution forces.

BUFFALO BILL
FRONTIERSMAN
1846-1917

William Frederick Cody claimed that he got the nickname Buffalo Bill by killing more than 4,000 buffalo in order to supply meat to a railroad company. From 1868 to 1872, Cody served as a scout for the U.S. Army. After a battle with Native Americans, he won a Congressional Medal of Honor—the highest U.S. military award.

In 1872, Buffalo Bill became a showman. Buffalo Bill's Wild West Show toured throughout the U.S. and Europe for more than 30 years. It included a mock battle with Indians and featured such stars as sharpshooter Annie Oakley and Chief Sitting Bull.

Ralph Bunche
Statesman and Scholar
1904-1971

In 1950, Ralph Bunche became the first black person to win a Nobel Peace Prize. In June 1947, the United Nations (UN) asked him to help bring about peace between Israel and its Arab neighbors in the Middle East. Thanks to Bunche's diplomatic skills and persistence, both sides signed an agreement in August 1949 that stopped their fighting.

Bunche, who was orphaned in 1915, was a brilliant student. He became his high school's valedictorian, but was barred from the honor society because of his race.

After his success with the peace agreement, Bunche continued to work as a high-ranking official at the UN until his death. He also championed the cause of greater civil rights for African Americans.

LUTHER BURBANK
PLANT EXPERT
1849-1926

Although he had little more than a high school education, Luther Burbank became the world's most famous plant breeder. He specialized in creating hybrids—plants produced by cross-breeding two different kinds of plants. For instance, a hybrid called the russett Burbank potato is now the most common potato sold in the U.S.

Burbank wanted to help boost world food production. He created more than 800 new types of trees, vegetables, fruits, flowers, and grasses at his California farm. All were bred to be tougher and better than the plants they had come from. Burbank's work popularized the use of hybrids.

Dick Button
Skating Champion
1929-

Dick Button is perhaps the greatest of all U.S. ice skaters. He won five world championships between 1948 and 1952. He also won gold medals at the 1948 and 1952 Winter Olympic Games. At the 1952 Olympics, he became the first skater ever to nail a triple jump in competition.

Button has worked hard to popularize ice skating. In the 1960s, he successfully encouraged television networks to broadcast amateur skating competitions. Button has served as a TV commentator for skating events, and won a 1981 Emmy for his work.

Admiral Richard E. Byrd
Polar Explorer
1888-1957

Admiral Richard E. Byrd did more than any other person to explore the frozen continent of Antarctica during the first half of the 20th century. Between 1928 and 1957, he led five expeditions there. As a result of these trips, huge sections of the continent were discovered and mapped. In 1934, he spent a winter alone at a weather station deep in Antarctica.

Byrd was a pioneering aviator. In 1929, he and a co-pilot became the first people to fly over the South Pole. The two men also claimed to have flown over the North Pole in 1926. They were awarded the Congressional Medal of Honor, but scholars now doubt that they actually passed over the pole.

Julius Caesar
Conqueror
100 B.C.-44 B.C.

Julius Caesar was one of the great generals and politicians of ancient times. However, his driving ambition helped destroy Rome's republican-style government—a system in which power was controlled by a group of senators, not by a king or emperor.

In 49 B.C., Caesar's many military victories had made him popular with the common people. The Senate, which was run by the city's wealthiest families, suspected that Caesar was plotting to become sole ruler. Senators tried to have him arrested, but that sparked a civil war. Caesar quickly won and became sole dictator of Rome.

Caesar stopped corruption and helped poor people. Even so, Roman senators assassinated him in an effort to restore the republic. Caesar's death sparked another civil war—one that ended the republic for good. For many centuries after Caesar, Rome was ruled by emperors.

ANDREW CARNEGIE
STEEL BARON
1835-1919

Andrew Carnegie *(KAR-nuh-gee)* lived the American dream. His family immigrated to the U.S. from Scotland when he was 12. Desperately poor, he worked in a variety of jobs, including a railroad company. Every penny that he earned, he later invested in steel companies.

By 1900, Carnegie controlled the entire steel industry and was worth about $100 billion in today's money. In 1892, some of Carnegie's workers went on strike and were killed in fighting with company guards. Many people blamed the violence on Carnegie's greed. However, he spent the last two decades of his life giving away his fortune, much of it to build public libraries.

Lewis Carroll
Author
1832-1898

Lewis Carroll was the pen name of Charles Lutwidge Dodgson, a mathematics professor at Oxford University, England. Carroll loved children and often gave parties for them. During one such party, he began telling a fantasy-filled story to Alice Liddell, the daughter of a family friend. He wrote the story down and, in 1864, published it as *Alice's Adventures in Wonderland*. In 1871, he published the sequel, *Through the Looking Glass*. Both books fascinate adults as well as children, because their silliness often masks deeper meanings.

Kit Carson
Frontiersman
1809-1868

At just five feet, six inches tall, Christopher "Kit" Carson did not look like one of the greatest scouts in the Wild West—but that is what he was. He ran away from home at age 14 to become a mountain man. Later, he teamed with an explorer named John C. Frémont. Frémont's stories about the great scout's calmness and bravery made Carson famous.

Carson had enough true adventures for an army of men. He fought Indians, blazed trails though deserts, and survived grizzly bear attacks. Still, cheap novels of the time made up tall tales about him. About one story, he said, "That thar may be true, but I ain't got no recollection of it."

Rachel Carson
Champion of Nature
1907-1964

Rachel Carson is best known for her 1962 book *Silent Spring*, which warns about pollution caused by pesticides. It showed readers how pesticides not only kill harmful insects, they can contaminate food and poison the environment. *Silent Spring* alarmed many people into taking action against pollution, which brought about changes in the way chemicals are used. With that one book, Carson almost single-handedly sparked the environmental movement, leading to even greater reforms around the world.

Carson fell in love with the sea and wildlife as a child. She became a marine biologist for the U.S. government, and wrote several books about the sea. She never knew how much her work helped change the world— she died only two years after *Silent Spring* was published.

Howard Carter
Discoverer of King Tut's Tomb
1873-1939

In 1922, Howard Carter, an English archaeologist, was running out of time and money. He had been digging in the Egyptian desert for years, looking for a royal tomb that had not been robbed. No untouched tomb had ever been found before, but Carter was sure that he could do it.

Just as his financial backing was drying up, Carter uncovered the tomb of Pharaoh Tutankhamen. Though slightly vandalized, Tut's treasure-filled tomb was mostly intact. The discovery thrilled researchers and showed the world how wealthy ancient Egypt had been.

Enrico Caruso
Opera Star
1873-1921

Born in Naples, Italy, the 18th of 21 children in a poor family, Enrico Caruso *(kuh-ROO-soh)* grew up to become one of the world's greatest opera singers. According to some people, he was the greatest opera singer of all time. Caruso had a ringing tenor voice that left audiences gasping in admiration.

As a boy, Caruso sang in church choirs and on streets corners. He did not begin formal singing lessons until he was 18, but his voice soon won him important roles in operas all over Europe and North and South America. Crowds turned out to hear him, and he became the highest paid opera singer in the world.

Caruso was the first singing star to make phonograph records. Opera fans still buy and admire his records today.

George Washington Carver
Scientist and Inventor
1864-1943

Born a slave, Carver rose to become one the U.S.'s greatest agricultural scientists. Using a poorly funded laboratory at the Tuskegee Institute in Alabama, Carver created more than 280 products from peanuts and 150 from the sweet potato, including ink, candy, instant coffee, paint, soap, and cereal.

By doing so, Carver showed that such crops could be profitable for poor farmers in the South. At the time, most farmers relied on cotton, which quickly wore out the soil and was easily destroyed by insects. In 1921, Carver became famous for his research, and used that fame to promote racial harmony.

Mary Cassatt
Painter
1844-1926

I ALWAYS WANTED TO KNOW WHAT IT FELT LIKE!

In the late 1800s, Impressionist painting was a radical new art form. Impressionists deliberately made their works look hazy and less realistic. They wanted to show what the eye sees at a glance.

Mary Cassatt (kuh-SAT) was one of only a few female Impressionist painters. She became famous for her portraits of mothers and children. She also encouraged her wealthy friends to collect Impressionist art, which helped make it more respectable.

Fidel Castro
Leader of Cuba
1926-

Castro, the lawyer son of a wealthy Cuban landowner, turned his back on his upbringing and decided to fight for the rights of the downtrodden. In 1959, he and his rebel forces overthrew a corrupt dictator, and Castro has ruled Cuba ever since. He improved education, health, and housing for the working class. However, in the process he became a dictator himself, and has since ruled with an iron hand. His political opponents have faced imprisonment and death. Many Cubans who oppose Castro's rule have fled to the U.S. During the Cold War (1946-1989), U.S. leaders feared and despised Castro because he formed alliances with the Soviet Union, where the Communist Party controlled all aspects of people's lives. Since the Soviet Union collapsed in 1991, Castro has granted his people some religious and economic freedoms, and relations between Cuba and the U.S. have improved slightly.

Catherine the Great
Empress of Russia
1729-1796

Catherine, a German princess, married the crown prince of Russia at age 16. Once her husband became Russia's czar, or ruler, he proved weak and incompetent. Catherine and her supporters had him removed from office. Later, he was poisoned.

Catherine took over. During her 34-year reign as czarina, she built schools and hospitals, and promoted religious tolerance. Even so, she did little to help most Russians, who were oppressed by horrible poverty and injustice. Catherine was more effective at expanding Russia's borders by taking over parts of Poland and Turkey.

Miguel de Cervantes
Creator of *Don Quixote*
1547-1616

Born into a once-proud Spanish family, Cervantes (sur-VAHN-tees) grew up poor. He became a professional soldier, badly maiming his left hand in battle. Later, Cervantes was captured by pirates and made a slave. His five-year imprisonment ended after a group of priests paid his ransom.

With his family poorer than ever, Cervantes turned to writing to earn money. He never escaped poverty, but his book *Don Quixote (dahn kee-HOTE-ee)* is considered one of the greatest novels of western literature. It is a part-funny, part-tragic tale of an elderly nobleman who wishes that he were a Medieval knight. Throughout all his troubles, Cervantes was known for his easygoing wit and good humor.

Wilt Chamberlain
Basketball Star
1936-1999

Wilt "The Stilt" Chamberlain had a record-setting career in the National Basketball Association (NBA). Between 1959 and 1973, Wilton Norman Chamberlain played on two championship teams and made 13 All-Star appearances. "The Big Dipper," as he was also called, racked up 31,419 points in his career. Only Kareem Abdul-Jabbar scored more.

Chamberlain, who stood 7 feet, 1 inch, played for teams in Philadelphia and Los Angeles and set 46 NBA records. Probably his greatest achievement came in 1962, when he scored 100 points in a single game! Experts and fans believe that that record will never be equaled or beaten.

Charlie Chaplin
Filmmaker and Silent-Movie Star
1889-1977

Charlie Chaplin was the most famous star in silent pictures. He directed most of his own movies, and is credited with developing many early filmmaking techniques. He is best known for his role as "the Little Tramp," a big-hearted vagabond who was always in trouble. Audiences loved the Little Tramp because he was an underdog, and laughed at his misadventures because Chaplin was a master of comic timing.

Born in London, Chaplin had a troubled start in life. His parents, both music-hall performers, were very poor. His mother had a nervous breakdown and his father died when Charlie was five. He and his brother spent much of their childhood on the streets or in charity homes. Chaplin became a stage performer at age eight. While touring the U.S. with a theater group, he caught a Hollywood producer's eye. He signed with a film studio in 1913, and immediately became a hugely popular star. In 1975, Britain's queen knighted him as Sir Charles Spencer Chaplin.

Charlemagne
Medieval Ruler
742-814

Charlemagne (SHAR-luh-MAIN)—whose name means Charles the Great—was the most famous European leader of the Middle Ages. After the fall of the Roman Empire in 476 A.D., Europe became backward and uncivilized. Charlemagne united most of Western Europe and started a rebirth of learning and culture. Charlemagne could be harsh. When he conquered pagan lands, he forced people to accept Christianity at the point of a sword. However, he encouraged better farming, promoted education, and stimulated trade by coining money. Although Charlemagne's empire fell apart when he died, his revival of European culture had a lasting impact.

Geoffrey Chaucer
Writer of *The Canterbury Tales*
1340-1400

Chaucer (CHAW-sur) was England's most famous writer before William Shakespeare. His best-known work is *The Canterbury Tales*, a collection of stories written in poetic verse. The tales are told by a group of pilgrims on their way to a religious shrine. They poke fun at different aspects of English society.

Chaucer, who came from a well-to-do family, was highly educated for his time. He visited several countries and spoke at least five languages. Chaucer spent most of his life as a government official, prospering greatly. He died before finishing *The Canterbury Tales*.

Cesar Chavez
Labor Organizer
1927-1993

When Cesar Chavez (SAY-sar CHAH-vez) was 10 years old, his parents lost their farm in Arizona. The family was forced to become migrant farmworkers, traveling around the country picking crops. Chavez left school in the eighth grade to help his parents.

When he grew up, he began organizing farmworkers to help them get better pay and safer working conditions. The union that he helped found, the United Farm Workers of America, accomplished those goals and benefited thousands of workers. After Chavez died, he was awarded the Presidential Medal of Freedom, the highest civilian honor in the U.S.

Anton Chekhov
Playwright
1860-1904

Anton Chekhov planned to be a doctor. As a medical student, he began writing to help support his family. Eventually, he lost interest in medicine. He devoted more and more time to his writing, and became one of Russia's best young authors.

At first, Chekhov wrote short stories. Later, he wrote several plays, including *The Seagull*, *Uncle Vanya*, and *The Cherry Orchard*. They sealed his reputation as a great writer.

Chekhov's characters were usually decent people who felt that they were wasting their lives. Despite those feelings, they were unable to change for the better. Chekhov died of tuberculosis at the relatively young age of 44.

Chief Joseph
Leader of the Nez Perce Indians
1840-1904

Chief Joseph led one of the most famous retreats in history. In 1877, the Nez Perce were pushed into war by white settlers trying to take their land in northeastern Oregon. At first, Joseph's forces won battles. However, he realized that the U.S. Army would finally beat him, so he tried to escape with his people into Canada.

Joseph led men, women, and children almost 1,000 miles, fighting battles and seeking food the whole way. They surrendered just before reaching Canada. As they did, Joseph made this now-famous declaration: "Hear me, my chiefs, I am tired; my heart is sick and sad. From where the sun now stands, I will fight no more forever."

Winston Churchill
World War II Leader
1874-1965

V IS FOR VICTORY!

Sir Winston Churchill is a towering 20th-century figure. His greatest moment came during World War II. The armies of Nazi Germany were rampaging through Europe in May 1940 just as Churchill was named prime minister of Great Britain. Britons stood all alone against the Nazis, but Churchill declared, "We will never surrender." His leadership saw Great Britain through the crisis, and Germany was defeated five years later.

Churchill was also a great writer and painter. He won the 1953 Nobel Prize for literature, and many of his paintings now hang in art museums. Churchill remained active for almost all of his 90 years and was widely mourned when he died.

ROBERTO CLEMENTE
BASEBALL STAR AND HUMANITARIAN
1934-1972

HE'S GOING TO HIT A LONG ONE!

Roberto Clemente (cluh-MEN-tee) was in a league of his own. The star right fielder for the Pittsburgh Pirates helped guide his team to World Series victories in 1960 and 1971. In an 18-season career, he won 12 straight Gold Gloves for fielding and racked up a lifetime batting average of .317. He became the 11th major leaguer to get 3,000 hits.

Clemente was killed in a plane crash on his way to deliver food and medicine to earthquake victims in Nicaragua. In 1973, he became the first Hispanic player elected to baseball's hall of fame.

Cleopatra
Queen of Egypt
69-30 B.C.

Cleopatra VII is remembered as one of the most beautiful women in history. In fact, she was plain. However, she was highly intelligent, and she was a good ruler of Egypt. Her wit and charm won the hearts of two great Roman leaders, Julius Caesar and Mark Antony.

Cleopatra's relationship with Mark Antony became her downfall. The two of them schemed to become rulers of Rome, and they helped start a war in order to crush their opponents. The plan backfired: Cleopatra and Antony were defeated. Both committed suicide to avoid being captured by their enemies.

TY COBB
BASEBALL STAR
1886-1961

Tyrus Raymond Cobb was probably the most feared and hated man to play baseball. He was feared for his skill as a player. He played 24 seasons starting in 1905. In that time, Cobb made 4,191 hits, a record that stood until 1985. He is third on the list for career stolen bases with 892.

Despite his success as an athlete, Cobb was a sad, angry man. His Detroit Tigers teammates despised his arrogance and temper. He also used dirty tricks against opponents, such as sliding into base with his spikes up. Even so, Cobb became one of the first five players elected to baseball's Hall of Fame in 1936.

Christopher Columbus
Explorer
1451-1506

In 1492, Christopher Columbus set out from Spain with three ships and sailed westward. He hoped to find a water route to Asia, but never achieved that goal. Instead, he came upon the Caribbean Islands of North America. According to his maps, they should not have been there, so he believed that he had arrived in India. It was one of the most important accidents in history.

Columbus—born in Genoa, Italy—was not the first European to reach the Americas. Vikings had reached the continent about 500 years before. However, most Europeans knew nothing of the Vikings' explorations. Columbus's discovery contributed a great deal to an accurate view of Earth's geography, and opened "the New World" to exploration—and exploitation—by Europe.

Nadia Comaneci
Olympic Gymnast
1961-

Nadia Comaneci *(NAHD-yah KOH-mahn-EECH)* of Romania became the first gymnast to score a perfect 10 in the Olympic Games. Her triumph occurred during the 1976 Olympics in Montreal, Canada. In all, she scored seven perfect 10s to win three gold medals, one silver, and one bronze.

Comaneci became a media sensation, even though she was from a communist country that was hostile to the U.S. At the 1980 Olympics in Moscow, she won two more gold medals as well as two silver medals. Comaneci is considered one of the greatest gymnasts of all time.

CONSTANTINE THE GREAT
EMPEROR
A.D. 272-337

Confucius
Philosopher
551-479 B.C.

Confucius *(kun-FYOO-shuhs)* is the most celebrated Chinese philosopher. He was born at a time of great disorder and bloodshed. China's Chou dynasty was crumbling and rival warlords fought constantly. Confucius's philosophy aimed to bring order and harmony to people and society.

Confucius tried to make people feel morally responsible for their actions. He also believed that a ruler should set an example by being good and wise. His teachings caught on around 100 B.C. and remained the most important force in Chinese life until about 1900. They are still a major influence.

Constantine was the first Roman emperor to convert to Christianity. Shortly before his reign, Christians had been viciously persecuted. With Constantine's conversion, though, Christianity became the official religion of the empire. Constantine allowed other religions to be practiced. However, he laid the foundation for Christianity's dominance in Europe.

After Constantine moved his capital from Rome to Constantinople (now called Istanbul), Rome and western Europe declined in importance. Meanwhile, the great city of Constantinople (in what today is Turkey) became the heart of the new Byzantine Empire, which lasted until the 1400s.

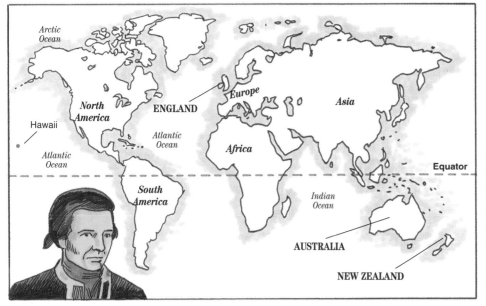

James Cook
Explorer
1728-1779

Captain James Cook said that his goal was "not only to go farther than anyone had done but as far as possible for man to go." One of history's greatest explorers, he came close to doing it. Cook was the first European to visit Hawaii, New Zealand, and Australia's east coast. He almost was the first to reach Antarctica; ice forced him to turn back.

Cook carried out three expeditions to the Pacific between 1768 and 1776. His travels led to the creation of European colonies throughout the region. Cook was killed in Hawaii, in a dispute over a boat.

Peter Cooper
Inventor and Philanthropist
1791–1883

As a teenager, Peter Cooper liked to invent things. While apprenticed to a wagon maker, he created a device that shaped wheel hubs. It was still in use when he died. Cooper made his fortune from a glue factory he bought in New York City. He used his wealth to invent America's first steam locomotive, develop the steel industry, and to lay the first transatlantic telegraph cable.

Cooper also used his money to help people by improving water supplies and police protection. Almost illiterate himself, he was an outspoken champion of public education. In 1859, he founded New York's Cooper Union, which taught art, science, and engineering for free.

I BUILT THIS "TOM THUMB" STEAM LOCOMOTIVE. ALL ABOARD!

Nicolaus Copernicus
Groundbreaking Astronomer
1473-1543

When Nicolaus Copernicus (*NIK-uh-LAY-us koh-PER-nih-kus*) was alive, most people believed that the sun and all other planets revolved around Earth. That theory had first been expressed by the Greek astronomer Ptolemy 1,400 years earlier. It was reinforced by Bible verses that spoke of the sun moving around Earth.

In 1543, Copernicus, a Polish priest and astronomer, suggested that this was all wrong. He published a book showing how Earth and the other planets revolved around the sun. Copernicus could not prove his theory, but later astronomers took up his work and proved him correct.

Hernán Cortés
Conqueror
1485-1547

Not long after Columbus discovered the Americas, Spanish *conquistadores* (conquerors) arrived from Europe to claim land and gold. One of the most famous was Hernán (or Hernando) Cortés *(hair-NAHN kore-TEZ)*. He took over the huge Aztec empire—land that is now Mexico.

Although greatly outnumbered, Cortés had three advantages. First, his men had guns and steel weapons, which the Aztecs lacked. Second, he made friends with a rival group of Indians, who helped him because they hated the powerful Aztecs. Third, European diseases such as smallpox—never seen in the New World—killed thousands of Aztecs. Two years after landing in 1519, Cortés was master of the Aztecs.

Bill Cosby
Pioneering Entertainer
1937-

Bill Cosby is a show-business pioneer and one of the most popular entertainers in the U.S. In 1965, he became the first black actor to star in a television drama on *I Spy*. In 1984, he launched *The Cosby Show*, a situation comedy that became the most watched TV show of the 1980s.

Cosby started as a stand-up comedian in the early 1960s. His warm-hearted humor made him popular with whites as well as blacks—rare for a black comedian at that time. He has written best-selling humor books and earned a doctorate in education.

Pierre de Coubertin
Founder of the Modern Olympics
1863-1937

The original Olympics began in ancient Greece, but were stopped around A.D. 400. Coubertin struggled against apathy and long odds to launch the first modern Olympiad in 1896. Only 14 countries—most of them European—participated.

Coubertin, a French baron, became president of the International Olympic Committee (IOC) in 1896 and held that post until 1925. Without his determination, the Olympics—which now hosts the teams of 190 countries—would not have continued. Following Coubertin's wishes, after his death his heart was buried in Olympia, Greece, the town for which the Olympics were named.

43

Jacques-Yves Cousteau
Oceanographer
1910-1997

During the 1960s and 1970s, Jacques-Yves Cousteau (*ZHAHK-eev koo-STOH*) became a celebrity in the U.S. because of his television show, *The Undersea World of Jacques Cousteau*. However, Cousteau, a former French navy captain, had already made a name for himself as an oceanographer. In 1943, he helped invent the aqualung, a device that lets divers breath underwater. He also invented several devices designed to let divers explore more freely.

Cousteau strongly opposed efforts to use the seas as a dumping ground for waste. In his books, movies, and TV shows, he tried to increase people's appreciation for the fragile ocean environment.

THAT'S HIM!

Crazy Horse
Oglala Sioux Chief
1844-1877

Crazy Horse was one of the most brilliant of all Indian warriors. He led several successful attacks against the U.S. Army. In 1876, he led the Sioux and Cheyenne to victory over General George Custer's force at the Battle of Little Bighorn in Montana. Custer and all his men were killed.

However, Crazy Horse's genius for battle could not stop the wave of white settlers and soldiers arriving in the West. In 1877, he surrendered. Later that year, he was killed by a soldier while being taken from his jail cell.

Today, sculptors in South Dakota are carving a huge statue of Crazy Horse into the side of a mountain. When completed, it will be taller than the Washington Monument in Washington, D.C., and larger than the Great Sphinx at Giza, Egypt.

David Crockett
Frontiersman
1786-1836

After Daniel Boone, "Davy" Crockett is America's most famous backwoodsman. Crockett ran away from home at age 13 to avoid being punished for getting into a fight. He later became a scout for the U.S. Army and fought against the Creek Indians. However, he protested against efforts to force Indians off their lands.

Crockett became a living legend in Tennessee. He charmed people with his coonskin cap, his rifle "Betsy," and his folksy way of "spinning yarns" (telling stories). Crockett served three terms in Congress, but was defeated in the 1834 election. He died defending the Alamo in a fight between Texans and Mexicans.

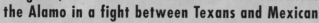

Walter Cronkite
TV News Anchor
1916-

During the 1960s and 1970s, Walter Cronkite was *the* source of news for most people in the U.S. As anchor of *The CBS Evening News*, Cronkite's deep, reassuring voice and professional manner won him the reputation of being "the most trusted man in America."

Cronkite began his journalism career working for wire services and served as a war correspondent during World War II (1939-1945). He moved to CBS in 1950 and helped launch *The CBS Evening News* in 1962. Cronkite anchored the program until his retirement in 1981. He left with his trademark signoff: "And that's the way it is."

Marie Curie
Nobel Prize-winning Scientist
1867-1934

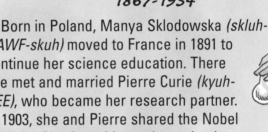

Born in Poland, Manya Sklodowska *(skluh-DAWF-skuh)* moved to France in 1891 to continue her science education. There she met and married Pierre Curie *(kyuh-REE)*, who became her research partner. In 1903, she and Pierre shared the Nobel Prize for Physics with another scientist for the discovery of radioactivity.

In 1911, Marie Curie became the first person ever to win a second Nobel Prize, this time in chemistry. Her brilliant work made her one of the most famous scientists of the 20th century. She died of leukemia caused by her prolonged exposure to radioactivity.

George Armstrong Custer
Army General and Indian Fighter
1839-1876

During the U.S. Civil War (1861-1865), Custer was the North's most dashing soldier. He earned a reputation as a fearless cavalry commander, but he was also widely hated for his arrogance. After the war, he was sent out west to fight Native Americans.

Like all Army officers, Custer was under pressure to defeat the Indians. In 1868, by the Washita River in Oklahoma, he led a massacre of Native American men, women, children. Eight years later, he recklessly attacked a huge Indian encampment in Montana, near the Little Bighorn River. That time, however, he and all 210 of his men were surrounded and killed at "Custer's Last Stand."

Vasco da Gama
Explorer
1469-1524

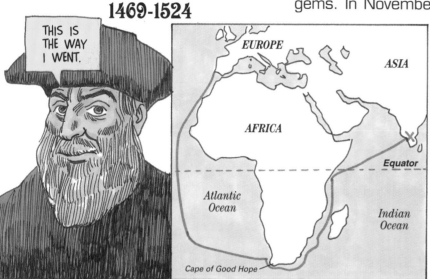

THIS IS THE WAY I WENT.

EUROPE

ASIA

AFRICA

Equator

Atlantic Ocean

Indian Ocean

Cape of Good Hope

In 1497, Portuguese sea captain Vasco da Gama was asked by his king to find a sea route to India. The king wanted to be able to trade for India's spices and precious gems. In November of that year, da Gama sailed around the southern tip of Africa and reached India about seven months later. He was the first to ever do so.

The journey was difficult. Arab traders in India feared Portuguese competition, and did everything they could to sabotage da Gama. Then, on the return trip, most of his sailors died of disease. However, da Gama's discovery of an all-water route between Europe and Asia greatly boosted the connection between the two continents.

Dalai Lama
Spiritual Leader
1935-

Most Tibetans are Buddhists, and recognize the Dalai Lama *(DAHL-ee LAH-muh)* as their spiritual and political leader. In 1940, young Tenzin Gyatso was enthroned as Dalai Lama—the 14th Dalai Lama since the A.D. 1200s. In 1950, China invaded Tibet, forcing the Dalai Lama into exile in neighboring India. Since then, he has tried to win Tibet's independence from China through peaceful means. His nonviolent efforts earned him the 1989 Nobel Peace Prize.

Louis Daguerre
Photography Pioneer
1878-1851

In the 1820s, Joseph Niepce *(nyeps)* created the first photographs. However, his process took eight hours to make a single fuzzy image. Fellow Frenchman Louis Daguerre *(duh-GAIR)* struggled for years to improve upon Niepce's work. In 1839, he did it: He came up with the first practical way to take sharp photographs in just minutes.

Daguerre's invention—an image on silver-plated copper—caused a worldwide sensation. It allowed ordinary people to preserve images quickly and cheaply. The daguerreotype, as it was called, remained the most popular type of photo until the 1850s. After that, more reliable types of photography came into use.

Clarence Darrow
Crusading Attorney
1857-1938

Clarence Darrow was the most famous criminal defense attorney of the 20th century. He championed organized labor and other liberal causes. Darrow's biggest trials came in the 1920s. In 1924, he saved two notorious killers, Nathan Leopold and Richard Loeb, from the death penalty by showing that they were insane. Both were sentenced to life in prison instead.

In 1925, Darrow defended John Scopes, a schoolteacher charged with violating Tennessee's law against teaching the theory of evolution (see *DARWIN, below*). Darrow lost the trial to his opponent, a famous politician named William Jennings Bryan. However, the trial made ordinary citizens begin to question the position of antievolutionists.

Charles Darwin
Naturalist
1809-1882

Many scientists before Charles Darwin had argued that plants and animals had evolved (gradually changed) over billions of years. Darwin, however, pinpointed how the process, which he called natural selection, works. Over time, living organisms are changed by their environments. The ones that adapt most successfully live to reproduce and pass their traits on to their offspring. Those less successful at adapting die off. Over billions of years, the best traits survive.

Darwin's ideas changed science and challenged religious beliefs. People who believe that all life was created in a short time by God have refused to accept evolution. Darwin's ideas are widely accepted in most countries, but they still arouse protests in the U.S.

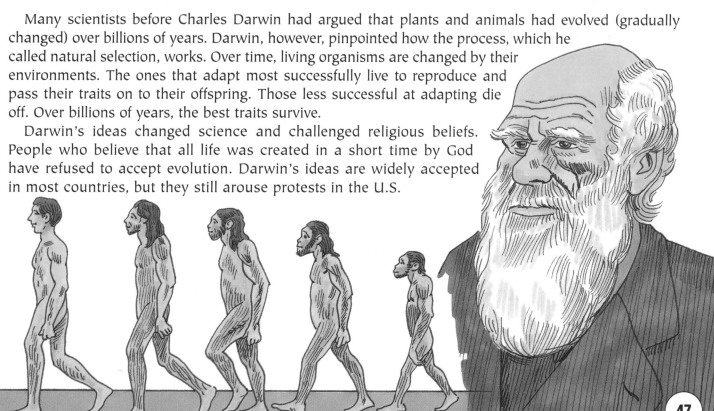

Leonardo da Vinci
Renaissance Genius
1452-1519

Leonardo da Vinci (*duh VIN-chee*) lived during a time called the Renaissance, which means "rebirth." It was the rebirth of the arts and sciences after their neglect during the Middle Ages. Leonardo was one of the leading figures of the Renaissance.

Leonardo created some of the most famous paintings in history, including *La Gioconda* (better known as the *Mona Lisa*) and *The Last Supper*. His artwork broke new ground with its graceful style and influenced all later artists.

Leonardo was also a great scientist, making advances in anatomy, engineering, and astronomy. Today, a person like Leonardo, who masters several different fields, is called a "Renaissance man."

Jefferson Davis
President of the Confederacy
1808-1889

Jefferson Davis was president of the Confederacy during the U.S. Civil War (1861-1865). He was trusted by the different political groups in the Confederate government. However, he could be very aloof, and often did a poor job of picking generals. After the war, many people unfairly blamed him entirely for the South's loss.

Davis was imprisoned for treason against the U.S. from 1865 to 1867. In 1877, he moved back to his native Mississippi. Davis lived out his life there and wrote his memoirs, *The Rise and Fall of the Confederate Government*. His birthday, June 3, is still a legal holiday in several southern states.

Benjamin O. Davis Jr.
World War II Airman
1912-

Davis's father was the first African American to be promoted to the rank of general in the U.S. Army. The younger Davis followed in his father's footsteps by attending the Army's military academy at West Point. Because he was black, Davis endured four years of silence from his fellow cadets. Still, he graduated with honors in 1936, the first African American to make it through West Point in the 20th century.

During World War II, Davis organized the Tuskegee Airmen, an all-black squadron. He flew 60 missions and was awarded the Distinguished Flying Cross. After the war, Davis became the first black general in the U.S. Air Force.

Eugene V. Debs
Labor Leader
1855-1926

In 1893, Eugene V. Debs organized the American Railway Union—an organization aimed at protecting the rights of railway workers. A year later, he launched a strike against the railroads over poor working conditions. The strike was broken by President Grover Cleveland, and Debs was thrown in jail for a while. However, he emerged as one of the country's top spokespersons for labor.

Debs, a committed socialist, believed that capitalism was an unfair, unequal system. His motto was, "When I rise, it will be *with* the ranks, not *from* the ranks." Debs ran for president five times on the Socialist ticket. In 1920, he ran while still in prison for making an antiwar speech during World War I (1914-1918). He got one million votes, a strong showing.

Jack Dempsey
Boxing Champion
1895-1983

CHARLES DE GAULLE
FRENCH PATRIOT AND PRESIDENT OF FRANCE
1890-1970

Outside of France, Charles de Gaulle is best remembered for his activities during World War II (1939-1945). He led the Free French forces after Nazi Germany conquered France in 1940. From their bases in Great Britain, the Free French eventually helped liberate France and the rest of Europe in 1945. After the war, de Gaulle became a towering figure in French politics. His main contributions were to stabilize France's government, which changed leadership every few months. He also brought together widely different political groups so that they could work together peaceably, and he increased France's prestige abroad.

Jack Dempsey—known as "the Manassa Mauler"—was one of the toughest and most popular boxers ever. He reigned as heavyweight champion from 1919 to 1926. He lost his title when challenger Gene Tunney upset him in a 10-round fight. In a rematch a year later, Dempsey knocked Tunney down, but forgot to stand in a corner of the ring while the referee counted to ten. The referee asked Dempsey to do so, then kept counting. Some say that gave Tunney a few extra seconds to get up; he did, and later won the fight. People still believe that the "Long Count" unfairly doomed Dempsey.

William Harrison Dempsey was born in Manassa, Colorado. He worked in copper mines, and it was in mining camps that he began boxing. Dempsey's pro career started in 1912. He retired with a record of 62 wins (49 of them knockouts), 6 losses, and 10 draws.

René Descartes
Founder of Modern Philosophy
1596-1650

I THINK, THEREFORE I AM.

René Descartes (*ruh-NAY day-KART*) was a great mathematician who invented analytic geometry. However, his main contribution to learning came in philosophy. He is often called the first modern philosopher because many of the issues that he raised are still at the heart of all philosophical debate.

Descartes wondered how we could be certain that anything exists. How do we know that we aren't just dreaming or being fooled by some evil genius? His answer was that we can at least be sure that we have thoughts, and that must mean that we exist. Descartes summed this up with his famous phrase, "I think, therefore I am."

Hernando de Soto
Conqueror and Explorer
1496-1542

Hernando de Soto made his fortune during Spain's conquest of Peru in 1532. He returned to Spain with a king's ransom in gold. However, he became restless in Spain. In 1539, De Soto led a 600-man expedition to what today is Florida. They became the first Europeans to discover the Mississippi River and to explore the southeastern U.S.

De Soto tortured Indians to find out where they hid their gold. This made the Spanish many enemies, and they were frequently attacked. De Soto died of fever, and only half his men made it safely to Mexico in 1543. The expedition never found any gold.

Diana, Princess of Wales
British Royalty
1961-1997

On July 29, 1981, an estimated one billion people watched on television as 19-year-old Diana Spencer married Prince Charles, heir to the British throne. Diana became an international celebrity whose hair, clothing, and makeup styles set trends. Her two young sons were also widely admired. In 1996, however, the marriage ended in a bitter divorce.

Diana continued to use her public position to focus attention on social issues, such as poverty, AIDS, and the loss of human life caused by land mines. In August 1997, the world was stunned to hear that Diana, only 36, had died in a Paris car crash.

Charles Dickens
Novelist
1812-1870

Charles Dickens is the author of some of the best-loved books in the English language, including *A Christmas Carol*, *A Tale of Two Cities*, and *Oliver Twist*. Just before Charles turned 12, his father was imprisoned for debt. The boy was sent to work in a factory, pasting labels on bottles. That experienc scarred him deeply and played a role in many of the books he later wrote.

Dickens first tasted success as an author at age 24, when he published *The Pickwick Papers*. His novels have memorable characters and are enjoyable to read. They also expose the needless cruelty faced by poor people of his era.

Emily Dickinson
Poet
1830-1886

Emily Dickinson is considered one of the greatest of all American poets, but only six of her poems were published in her lifetime. She was a recluse, spending her life in her parents' house. She never married, seldom had visitors, and rarely went outdoors. Because of these habits, we know little about her.

Her 1,700 poems are well-known, though—for the short, sharp observations that they make about life, death, love, and God. Apparently, Dickinson did not want her poems made public. After her death, her sister discovered them and had them published.

Rudolf Diesel
Inventor of the Diesel Engine
1858-1913

Most trucks, buses, trains, and ships owe their get-up-and-go to Rudolf Diesel, a German mechanic. Diesel wanted to invent an engine that would be more efficient than steam- or gasoline-powered engines. It took him 13 years, but in 1892, he created one that ran on oil. The device made him wealthy.

Diesel engines are suited for heavy work because they can haul more than gasoline engines of the same size. Also, the fuel is generally cheaper than gasoline.

In 1913, Diesel mysteriously disappeared from a ship in the English Channel, and was presumed drowned.

Joe DiMaggio
Baseball Star
1914-1999

During the 1941 season, Joe DiMaggio of the New York Yankees set a baseball record by hitting safely in 56 consecutive games. It was the greatest achievement of his awesome 15-year career. DiMaggio had a lifetime batting average of .325, and he led the Yankees to the World Series 10 times before retiring in 1951. Joseph Paul DiMaggio, called "Joltin' Joe" or "the Yankee Clipper" by his fans, is remembered for his graceful yet powerful playing style.

In 1954, DiMaggio was briefly married to Marilyn Monroe, a famous actor and screen idol.

WALT DISNEY
CREATOR OF MICKEY MOUSE
1901-1966

WHAT ABOUT PLUTO?

AND MINNIE MOUSE!

DON'T FORGET DONALD DUCK!

AND GOOFY!

AND THE 101 DALMATIANS!

In the 1920s, Walter Elias Disney was a struggling cartoonist. After five years of trying, he scored his first success in 1928 with a cartoon featuring Mickey Mouse. The filmmaker went on to make such classic films as *Bambi*, *The Lady and the Tramp*, *Snow White*, *Pinocchio*, and *Fantasia*.

In 1955, Disney opened the first Disneyland theme park in California. Other Disney parks have since opened in Florida and in foreign countries, such as France and Japan. The Walt Disney Co. is now one of about 10 giant companies that control most types of news and entertainment in the United States.

Fyodor Dostoevsky
Novelist
1821-1881

Fyodor Dostoevsky (*FYAW-dahr DAHS-tuh-YEF-skee*) created brooding novels that made him one of Russia's greatest writers. All of his works explore inner struggles, especially the battle between good and evil in all people.

Dostoevsky's own life was full of struggle. Political opponents had him imprisoned for eight months and sentenced to die, but spared his life at the last moment. Dostoevsky gambled heavily, and had trouble holding on to money. Dostoevsky believed that life is a mystery that demands to be explored. At age 18, he wrote: "I occupy myself with this mystery, because I want to be a man."

Frederick Douglass
Civil-rights Pioneer
1818?-1895

Frederick Douglass's speeches against slavery made him the most prominent black American before the U.S. Civil War (1861-1865). Douglass was born a slave in Maryland, and given the name Frederick Bailey. One of his masters helped teach him to read, even though it was against the law to teach reading to slaves. At age 20, Bailey escaped to freedom in the north.

As a free man, he changed his name to Douglass. In 1841, he was catapulted to fame after giving a powerful speech about his slave experiences. In 1845, he wrote an autobiography, *Narrative of the Life of Frederick Douglass.* After the war, Douglass remained an outspoken champion of equal rights for blacks.

Arthur Conan Doyle
Creator of Sherlock Holmes
1859-1930

Arthur Conan Doyle started his career as a doctor, but he couldn't drum up many patients. So he began writing Sherlock Holmes stories to pass the time. The "world's greatest detective" became a hit in 1887, and Doyle became an international celebrity.

In 1893, Doyle tried to kill off Sherlock Holmes in order to focus on other types of writing. However, Holmes's "death" prompted street protests in London and a huge outcry around the world. Doyle finally revived his superhero, but spent most of his later years obsessed with efforts to communicate with the dead.

I DO THE WORK; HE TAKES THE CREDIT!

Charles Drew
Medical Pioneer
1904-1950

In the 1930s, Charles Drew became one of the top experts in the United States in using blood to save lives. His research helped discover the best ways to store blood and plasma, a useful part of blood. During World War II, when blood was in high demand, the blood banks he started saved thousands of lives.

Drew, an African American, succeeded despite widespread prejudice. Although his skin and hair were light enough to allow him to pass as white, Drew identified himself as black. He resigned from the Red Cross when he found out that it would not use blood from blacks to treat white patients.

W. E. B. Du Bois
Civil-rights Pioneer
1868-1963

William Edward Burghardt Du Bois *(doo-BOYS)* was the leading spokesman for black civil rights during the early 1900s. Du Bois was a strong opponent of the black educator Booker T. Washington. Washington believed that blacks could improve their standing mainly through hard work and education.

Du Bois said that African Americans must also agitate against the injustices they faced. His 1903 book *The Souls of Black Folk* was a rallying cry for black civil rights. Du Bois also helped to found the National Association for the Advancement of Colored People (NAACP). Late in life, he embraced communism and moved to the African country of Ghana.

BOB DYLAN
MUSICIAN
1941-

Isadora Duncan
Dancer
1877-1927

I WANT TO DANCE!

Dancers in the late 1800s were taught to follow many rules to do their craft. Isadora Duncan changed all that in 1898 when she began coming up with her own free-flowing dances. She tossed away items from the dancer's costume such as ballet shoes and tights, and based her moves on what she believed were ancient Greek dances. Her ideas had a big effect on modern dance.

Duncan was a free spirit, but lived a very troubled life. Though an American, she found her greatest success in Europe, and she traveled widely as a teacher and performer.

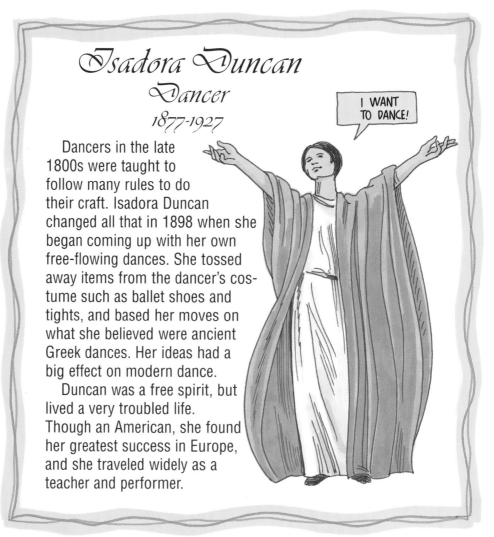

Aside from the Beatles, Bob Dylan was the most influential musician among young people during the 1960s. Dylan's songs, such as "Blowin' in the Wind" and "A Hard Rain's A-Gonna Fall" became theme songs for civil-rights and antiwar protesters.

Dylan (born Robert Allen Zimmerman) has a scratchy, nasal voice that is instantly recognizable. He started as a folk singer, but later branched out into rock and country. Some of his albums have become legendary, while others have been criticized for their poor quality. In 1989, he was inducted into the Rock and Roll Hall of Fame.

Amelia Earhart
Aviation Pioneer
1897-1937

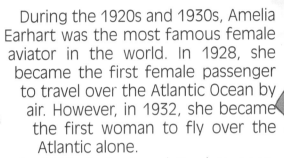

During the 1920s and 1930s, Amelia Earhart was the most famous female aviator in the world. In 1928, she became the first female passenger to travel over the Atlantic Ocean by air. However, in 1932, she became the first woman to fly over the Atlantic alone.

In 1937, Earhart and Fred Noonan, her navigator, tried to fly around the world. Near the end of their journey, their plane disappeared without a trace over the South Pacific. Countless efforts have been made to find the wreckage of Earhart's last flight, all without success.

Wyatt Earp
Western Lawman
1848-1929

Wyatt Earp (*urp*) was a principal player in the shoot-out at the O.K. Corral, probably the most famous gunfight in the American West. On one side of the showdown in Tombstone, Arizona, were the three Earp brothers—Wyatt, Virgil, and Morgan—and their friend Doc Holliday. On the other side were Billy and Ike Clanton, and Tom and Frank McLaury.

Billy Clanton and the McLaury brothers died in the 30-second gunfight; Ike Clanton survived. Many books, movies, and TV shows have portrayed the Earps as heroes. In truth, however, the shoot-out was a battle between two sets of shady characters seeking to settle a feud.

George Eastman
Photography Pioneer
1854-1932

In the late 1800s, photography was popular, but cameras were expensive, bulky, and complicated to use. George Eastman changed all that when he invented the Kodak Brownie camera. Each Brownie sold for one dollar and could take 100 photos. Once all the photos were taken, the owner sent the camera to Kodak to develop the pictures and reload the camera with new film. Eastman's slogan was "You press the button, we do the rest."

Eastman put cameras in the hands of ordinary people for the first time. Taking a picture became quick and easy. People compared it to firing off a gun, calling the new type of photos "snapshots."

Thomas A. Edison
Inventor
1847-1931

Electric light

Phonograph

Kinetoscope

Voting machine

35-mm film

Stock market ticker

Thomas Alva Edison was one of the greatest inventors of all time. In 1877, he invented the phonograph (record player) and, in 1879, he invented the first practical electric light bulb. Edison also introduced the first talking "moving picture" (movie with sound) and made major improvements in the telephone and the typewriter. In all, he patented 1,093 inventions.

Edison did not create all his inventions alone. His many assistants, who were experts in different fields, helped make his ideas possible. Edison defined genius as "1 percent inspiration and 99 percent perspiration." His genius resulted in inventions that revolutionized daily life.

Alexandre Gustave Eiffel
Designer of the Eiffel Tower
1832-1923

It is impossible to think of Paris without thinking of the Eiffel Tower. Completed in 1889 for that year's World's Fair, the 984-foot-tall tower became the tallest structure in the world. It held that honor until New York's Chrysler building topped it in 1930.

Eiffel, the man who created the tower, was a bridge builder who also designed the framework for the Statue of Liberty. After the 1889 World's Fair closed, some people wanted to tear down Eiffel's masterpiece. He came up with new uses for the tower, such as making it into a weather and telegraph station. Today, the Eiffel Tower is one of the world's most popular tourist attractions.

$$E = MC^2$$

Albert Einstein
Scientific Genius
1879-1955

Along with Sir Isaac Newton, Albert Einstein is considered the greatest scientist of all time. From 1905 to 1925, Einstein created a series of mathematical and scientific formulas and theories that radically changed the way scientists looked at space, time, gravity, and matter. All types of physics—the study of matter and energy—are shaped by Einstein's thinking.

Einstein won the Nobel Prize for his work in 1921. He is probably best remembered for creating theories that later made nuclear weapons possible. However, Einstein was a peaceful man who strongly opposed the use of such weapons.

Einstein's famous formula, E = mc², stands for "Energy equals mass times the velocity [speed] of light squared."

Dwight D. Eisenhower
U.S. General and 34th President
1890-1969

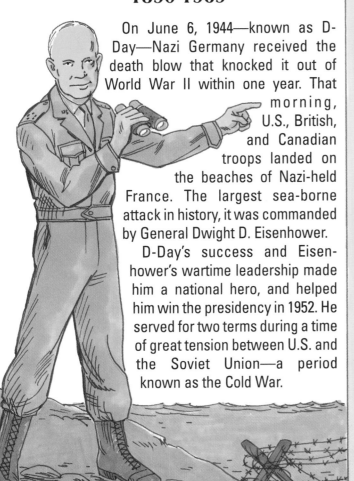

On June 6, 1944—known as D-Day—Nazi Germany received the death blow that knocked it out of World War II within one year. That morning, U.S., British, and Canadian troops landed on the beaches of Nazi-held France. The largest sea-borne attack in history, it was commanded by General Dwight D. Eisenhower.

D-Day's success and Eisenhower's wartime leadership made him a national hero, and helped him win the presidency in 1952. He served for two terms during a time of great tension between U.S. and the Soviet Union—a period known as the Cold War.

Elizabeth I
Queen of England
1533-1603

When 25-year-old Elizabeth Tudor took the throne in 1558, England had been nearly destroyed by fighting between Protestants and Catholics and serious financial trouble plagued the nation.

"Good Queen Bess," as she was called, shocked many people by refusing to marry and by guarding her power jealously. However, she used that power wisely, and the Elizabethan Age became a golden time for England.

By the end of Elizabeth's 45-year reign, England had become a mighty nation. Its power grew overseas, thanks to naval battles, and its wealth grew, thanks to trade. At home, writers such as William Shakespeare and Francis Bacon penned some of the greatest works of the English language.

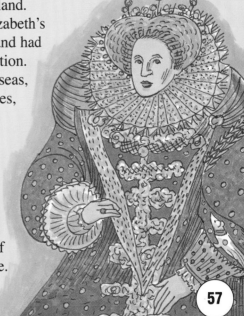

DUKE ELLINGTON
JAZZ MUSICIAN
1899-1974

Duke Ellington was one of the best known of all jazz composers and band leaders. Born Edward Kennedy Ellington, he was nicknamed Duke by his family. He learned to play piano mostly by listening to ragtime musicians in his hometown of Washington, D.C. By his early 20s, Ellington was a successful musician.

From 1927 to 1932, Ellington's band gained international fame at New York City's Cotton Club in Harlem. After that, his band toured frequently and created such hit songs as "Take the A Train" and "Sophisticated Lady." Ellington produced more than 1,500 musical works in his lifetime. In 1969, he was awarded the Presidential Medal of Freedom.

Ralph Ellison
Novelist
1914-1994

Ralph Ellison published only one novel in his lifetime: *Invisible Man*. However, it is one of the most influential of all books about the black experience in America.

The hero of Ellison's book is a young Southern black man who struggles to find his identity, first in his native South and then in the North. Ellison uses the character's experiences to show how racial prejudice can make it difficult for African Americans to develop a sense of dignity and worth.

Invisible Man was published in 1952 and won the National Book Award in 1953. Although the book appeared long before the civil-rights victories of the 1960s, many of the racial problems that it describes still exist in the U.S. today.

Leif Ericson
Warrior and Explorer
980-1025

Leif Ericson, a Viking, is widely believed to be the first European to discover North America. Born in Iceland and raised in Greenland, Leif was the son of Eric the Red, another Viking explorer. Around 1002, Ericson led an expedition of 35 men to look for a territory that had been spotted by the crew of a Viking ship.

Ericson's boat touched land in three different places, all of which historians believe to be along Canada's northeastern coast. After Ericson, other Vikings tried to establish a colony at one of those sites. It did not last long: Hostility from native people apparently forced the Vikings to leave. Archaeologists found the remains of that colony in 1963.

Euclid
Mathematician
330-270 B.C.

Euclid *(YOO-klid)* is called the "father of geometry." That is because he wrote a textbook about geometry called *Elements*. It would definitely win the prize for "longest continuously used math book"—people have used it to learn geometry for 2,000 years! Probably no other book has had such an impact on scientists and scientific thinking.

Very little is known about Euclid's life. We do know that he was a teacher in Alexandria, Egypt, and that he helped educate the king there. The difficulty of Euclid's book frustrated the king, who asked if there wasn't an easier way to study the subject. Euclid replied, "There is no royal road to geometry."

Euripides
Playwright
480-406 B.C.

Euripides *(yoo-RIP-uh-deez)* is one of three great tragic playwrights from ancient Greece. The other two are Sophocles *(SAHF-uh-kleez)* and Aeschylus *(ESS-kuh-lus)*. Euripides wrote more than 90 plays, though only 19 survive. Many of them deal with emotions, relationships, and other personal issues, as opposed to religious celebrations or victories in battle, which were the subjects of most plays in ancient Greece.

The plays that Euripides wrote were often unpopular during his lifetime. In many ways, he was centuries ahead of his time. He is one of the few ancient Greeks known to have questioned slavery, which was commonplace at that time. Also, unlike other playwrights, he often showed women—who were not considered equal to men—as strong, brave, and honorable.

Chris Evert
Tennis Star
1954-

Chris Evert dominated women's tennis through much of the 1970s. Her father was a tennis instructor, and she began playing when she was five years old. In 1970, as a 15-year-old, Evert defeated Margaret Court, the world's top-ranked women's player at the time. She turned pro in 1972, and four years later became the first woman in tennis to earn $1 million.

In the mid-1970s, Evert was ranked No. 1 for five consecutive years. She took home a record 157 singles titles and she captured at least one Grand Slam singles title for 13 years in a row. Evert won the U.S. Open six times and Wimbledon three times.

Philo Taylor Farnsworth
Inventor of Television
1906-1971

AND THERE IS STILL NOTHING TO WATCH!

Enrico Fermi
Helped Build the Atomic Bomb
1901-1954

During the 1930s, Enrico Fermi was one of the world's most brilliant nuclear physicists. His work earned him a Nobel Prize in 1938. However, Italy—his native country—had become a friend of Nazi Germany. In 1939, just as World War II was breaking out, Fermi escaped to the U.S.

During the war, Fermi was one of the key scientists working on the Manhattan Project, a huge U.S. effort to build an atomic bomb. He created the first man-made nuclear chain reaction, which proved that the bomb was possible. After the war, however, Fermi argued against making the hydrogen bomb and other more powerful weapons.

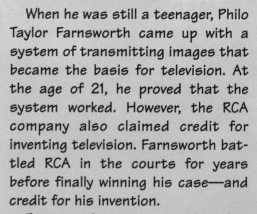

When he was still a teenager, Philo Taylor Farnsworth came up with a system of transmitting images that became the basis for television. At the age of 21, he proved that the system worked. However, the RCA company also claimed credit for inventing television. Farnsworth battled RCA in the courts for years before finally winning his case—and credit for his invention.

Farnsworth went on to do other important scientific work. However, he regretted creating TV, his most famous invention. As his son later recalled, "I suppose you could say that he felt he had created kind of a monster, a way for people to waste a lot of their lives."

ELLA FITZGERALD
SINGER
1917-1996

Beginning in the early 1940s, Ella Fitzgerald was considered "the first lady of song." She began her career at 16, when she won a talent contest at the famous Apollo Theater in Harlem. By the time she was 18, she had released her first hit song—a swinging version of a child's nursery rhyme, "A-Tisket, A-Tasket."

Fitzgerald had a crystal-clear voice with a remarkable range. She became known for "scat singing"—using her voice the way a musician uses an instrument, singing with sounds as well as words. She recorded more than 2,000 songs, sold more than 40 million records, and won 13 Grammy Awards, including one for lifetime achievement.

Alexander Fleming
Discoverer of Penicillin
1881-1955

In 1928, Alexander Fleming was a researcher studying deadly bacteria. A small bit of mold began growing on one of the bacteria cultures he left out. Most scientists would have thrown the culture away, but Fleming happened to notice that the bacteria around the mold had been killed off.

A decade later, other scientists used Fleming's discovery as the basis for the wonder drug, penicillin. Penicillin and other antibiotics kill bacteria, allowing doctors to treat many life-threatening diseases, including tuberculosis, pneumonia, and scarlet fever. As a tribute to the millions of lives saved by antibiotics, Fleming and the other scientists shared the 1945 Nobel Prize.

Margot Fonteyn
Ballet Star
1919-1991

Margot Fonteyn (*fahn-TAYN*) is considered one of the greatest ballerinas of the 20th century. Born Margaret Hookham, Fonteyn became a star at the age of 16 and soon reigned as the queen of British ballet. After World War II, she emerged as an international star.

Fonteyn's most famous moments came late in her career. In 1961, Rudolf Nureyev, a Russian ballet star, escaped from the Soviet Union and began dancing with Fonteyn. Their pairing was electric. It became one of the most famous in ballet, and lasted 15 years. In 1979, Britain's Royal Ballet gave Fonteyn the rare title of *prima ballerina assoluta*, meaning "absolutely the first [or top-ranking] ballerina."

Henry Ford
Carmaker and Business Pioneer
1863-1947

When Henry Ford got into the automobile business in 1896, cars were toys for rich people. Ford did two things to change that. First, he made a tough, reliable car called the Model T. Second, he streamlined the carmaking process by using an assembly line and by producing his own glass and steel.

Ford passed on his cost savings to customers and, by 1918, half of all U.S. cars were Model Ts. Ford was hailed as a genius, but he was also a controversial figure. For one thing, he fought all attempts by labor unions to organize in Ford Motor Company plants.

Dian Fossey
Champion of
African Gorillas
1932-1985

Dian Fossey was a zoologist who, in 1966, began living with mountain gorillas in eastern Africa, to study them. She continued to live with them in isolation for nearly 18 years, and became the world's foremost expert on their behavior. In 1983, she published her book *Gorillas in the Mist*, which became a best-seller.

Fossey also tried to protect the endangered gorillas from poachers (illegal hunters) and to protect the gorillas' habitat from farmers. This made her many enemies. In 1985, she was found murdered, apparently by poachers. In 1988, Hollywood released a popular movie based on her book.

Anne Frank
Holocaust Heroine
1929-1945

When Germany's Nazis invaded Holland in 1940, they began rounding up Jewish people to kill them. To avoid that fate, 13-year-old Anne Frank and her family went into hiding in a secret area of her father's office building. Anne and seven other people shared the small space for two years.

During this imprisonment, Anne kept a diary. When Anne's family's hideaway was discovered by the Nazis, they were taken to concentration camps, where Anne died. After the war, her diary was published under the title *Anne Frank: The Diary of a Young Girl*. Full of tremendous insight, her diary remains an international bestseller and a moving document of the Holocaust.

Benjamin Franklin
Founding Father
1706-1790

Even if Benjamin Franklin had not been one of the U.S. Founding Fathers, he would be well remembered. As a scientist, he invented the lightning rod, bifocal glasses, and a fuel-efficient wood-burning stove. In his adopted hometown of Philadelphia, he reformed the police, made sure the streets got cleaned, improved the mail system, printed a newspaper, and established libraries.

During the American Revolution, Franklin was responsible for winning France's help in the war. Later, he served at the Constitutional Convention and settled disputes that might have wrecked an agreement. When Franklin died, 20,000 mourners attended his funeral. He remains one of the most beloved Americans ever.

Sigmund Freud
Pioneering Psychiatrist
1856-1939

Sigmund Freud *(froyd)*, an Austrian doctor, helped to found the field of medicine known as psychiatry *(sye-KYE-uh-tree)*, the study of the human mind. He asserted that many human actions are caused by subconscious, or hidden, desires. For example, an accidental misstatement—now known as a *Freudian slip*—can reveal a person's true feelings.

Many of Freud's original ideas have since been proven wrong—some by Freud himself. However, Freud's influence is impossible to underestimate. Many of his terms—such as *ego* and *neurosis*—are now commonly used words. His ideas have influenced countless writers, artists, and scientists.

Betty Friedan
Feminist Movement Founder
1921-

In 1963, a book called *The Feminine Mystique*, written by Betty Friedan *(free-DAN)*, shocked the world. At that time, most women—even highly educated ones—were expected to be housewives who helped their husbands to succeed. Friedan questioned that role, saying that it confined many women to unfulfilling, unhappy lives.

Friedan's book is widely credited with helping to start the women's liberation movement of the 1960s. That movement led to major changes in the types of jobs that were open to women and in the way women were treated by men.

Robert Frost
Poet
1874-1963

Robert Frost was the most popular American poet of the 20th century. He became famous for simple, elegant poems such as "Stopping by Woods on a Snowy Evening" and "Mending Wall," but also wrote longer, more complex works. He won four Pulitzer Prizes for his work.

Frost could be a difficult man to live with, and his personal life was marred by untimely deaths and other tragedies. Still, he became America's most famous poet during his lifetime. The highlight of his career came in 1961, when he recited his poem "The Gift Outright" at President John F. Kennedy's inauguration.

Robert Fulton
Inventor of the Steamboat
1765-1815

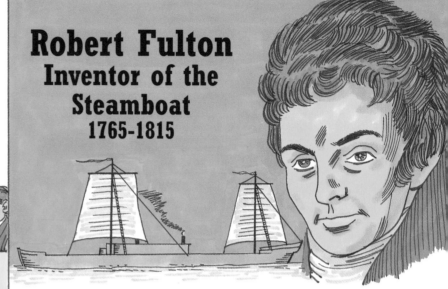

Robert Fulton is remembered for building the *Clermont*—the first commercially successful steam-powered boat. The *Clermont*'s success caused steamships to gradually replace less-reliable sailing ships. Steam power created a worldwide revolution in the way people and goods were transported.

Fulton began his career as a portrait painter. By 1793, however, he had become more interested in science and engineering. He worked first on canals, then on submarines. Almost a century before submarines became workable, Fulton built a "diving boat," which he named the *Nautilus*. It could descend 25 feet under water, rise to the surface, and blow up a target ship, but Fulton never worked out problems with its ability to move underwater.

Yuri Gagarin
First Human in Space
1934-1968

The year 1961 was a tense time in the Cold War between two superpowers, the U.S. and the Soviet Union. They were locked in a "space race" to see which would be first to put a person in space. On April 12, 1961, the Soviets won the race: A Soviet spacecraft called *Vostok 1* lifted off, carrying Yuri Gagarin, an air-force fighter pilot turned cosmonaut.

Gagarin—often called the Columbus of the Cosmos—became the first human to orbit Earth. His flight, which lasted 1 hour and 48 minutes, was his only space mission. He died when a fighter jet he was test-piloting crashed near Moscow. At the time of his death, he was training for a second space mission.

Galen
Doctor and Scientist
A.D. 129–210

Galen (GAY-lun) was one of the greatest healers in ancient times. Only the Greek doctor Hippocrates was more influential. Galen became an expert in anatomy, even though Roman religious beliefs banned cutting open and studying dead human bodies. Instead, Galen studied animal bodies. He also became a doctor to gladiators. Their horrible wounds gave him insights into the human anatomy.

Galen's writings influenced doctors for the next 1,500 years. He made many advances, such as correctly identifying the purposes of arteries (that they carry blood, not air) and the vocal cords. Though he also made mistakes that took centuries to correct, his teachings remain part of the foundation of Western medicine.

Galileo
Astronomer, Physicist, Mathematician
1564-1642

Galileo (gal-uh-LEE-oh) is best known for building the first astronomical telescope and using it to observe objects in space. In this way, he discovered four of Jupiter's moons and found that the Milky Way galaxy is made up of stars.

In Galileo's day, scientists and church leaders agreed that the sun revolved around Earth. However, Galileo agreed with Copernicus, a Polish astronomer, who believed the opposite: that Earth revolves around the sun.

Because Galileo disagreed with the teachings of the Roman Catholic Church, the Church forced him to give up his beliefs and submit to house arrest for the last eight years of his life. In 1984, the Church finally pardoned Galileo; in 2000, it apologized for his mistreatment.

Indira Gandhi
Prime Minister of India
1917-1984

Mohandas K. Gandhi
Founder of Modern India
1869-1948

INDIA

Indira Gandhi *(in-DEER-uh GAHN-dee)* was born into India's most important political family. Her father, Jawaharlal Nehru *(juh-WAH-hur-lahl NAY-roo)*, became India's prime minister after the country gained independence from Great Britain in 1947. Indira worked as his aide, which taught her a great deal about politics.

In 1966, Nehru died. Some of his political allies made Indira Gandhi prime minister, thinking that she would be easy to control. Instead, she used her power brilliantly and often ruthlessly. She served as prime minister twice, in 1966-1977 and in 1980-1984. She was assassinated by two of her bodyguards, who were members of the Sikh religion. They said that they were avenging an attack she had ordered on a holy Sikh site while trying to wipe out a group of terrorists who were hiding there.

Mohandas K. Gandhi *(moh-hun-DAS kay GAHN-dee)* was one of the most remarkable men of the 20th century. Using completely nonviolent means, he led the movement to win India's independence from Great Britain. In 1947, he achieved his goal against incredible odds. His movement's victory greatly influenced U.S. civil-rights leaders, most notably Martin Luther King Jr. Gandhi was called *Mahatma*, which means "great soul."

Gandhi (no relation to Indira Gandhi) also worked hard to achieve harmony among India's many religious and ethnic groups. After independence, vicious fighting broke out between Hindus, who make up a majority of all Indians, and Muslims. Gandhi—a Hindu—was assassinated by a Hindu religious fanatic who opposed religious tolerance.

Giuseppe Garibaldi
Italian Patriot
1807-1882

Bill Gates
Computer Billionaire
1955-

In 1975, William H. Gates III dropped out of Harvard University to found Microsoft, a company that created computer software. By 1983, Microsoft software was being used in 40 percent of all home computers, and the demand for home computers was exploding. In 1987, Gates became the world's youngest-ever billionaire at age 31.

Gates has been called a management genius for creating a casual yet challenging atmosphere for his employees. His biggest hurdle came in 2000, when a federal judge ruled that Microsoft had been using its power in the computer industry to destroy or hamper competitors.

Henry Louis Gates
Scholar and Historian
1950-

Henry Louis Gates played an important role in reviving the study of African American literature in the 1970s and 1980s. He has specialized in unearthing and publishing forgotten books and other writings by black Americans. He has also worked to increase appreciation for African culture and arts.

Gates is a professor at Harvard University and is director of Harvard's W. E. B. Du Bois Institute for Afro-American Research. There, Gates has brought together many of the country's top African American scholars. His books include *Thirteen Ways of Looking at a Black Man*, *Colored People: A Memoir*, and *The Norton Anthology of African American Literature*.

In the mid-1800s, the country that today is Italy was a collection of small kingdoms, many of them controlled by foreigners. Giuseppe Garibaldi *(juh-SEP-ee GAR-uh-BAWL-dee)* became part of a small group determined to throw off foreign rule and unite Italy under one government.

While the other patriots provided political efforts, Garibaldi supplied the military might. He was a brilliant leader, and he and his volunteer army of 1,000 "Redshirts" liberated large sections of the country. The Kingdom of Italy was proclaimed in 1861, but struggles continued for another decade. In 1870, Garibaldi led another group of volunteers into battle, this time in support of the French in the Franco-Prussian War.

Lou Gehrig
Baseball Star
1903-1941

From June 1, 1925, through April 30, 1939, Lou Gehrig, the New York Yankees' first baseman, was the "iron horse" of professional baseball. He played in 2,130 consecutive games on the Yankees regular season schedule. That record held until 1995, when it was broken by Cal Ripken Jr. of the Baltimore Orioles

Henry Louis Gehrig played that many games because he was that good. He had a lifetime batting average of .340 and was twice voted the American League's most valuable player. In 1939, he contracted amyotrophic lateral sclerosis (ALS), a rare and crippling nerve disorder. His departure from baseball is still regarded as one of the saddest events in the history of the game. Today, the illness that crippled and killed him is often called Lou Gehrig's disease.

Genghis Khan
Mongol Conqueror
1162-1227

I'M THE GREATEST!

In the early A.D. 1200s, Genghis Khan *(JEHNG-giss KAHN)* conquered a huge Asian empire reaching from the Pacific Ocean to the Black Sea. Born Temunjin, his father—the chief of several small tribes—died when he was 13. A rival chief took over the tribes, and for a while Temunjin and his family lived in poverty.

As a man, Temunjin's courage attracted many followers, and he assembled well-disciplined armies that conquered neighboring tribes. In 1206, he won the title *Genghis Khan*, which probably means "greatest of all rulers." After that, Genghis Khan went on to conquer China as well as parts of India and Europe.

George III
King of Great Britain
1738-1820

George III is widely remembered as the king whose tyranny sparked the American Revolution. American colonists thought that they were taxed too heavily, but George III stubbornly ignored their complaints. As a result, Great Britain lost its most valuable colonies. After that loss, the power of Great Britain's parliament (lawmakers) increased and the king's power decreased.

George III's 59-year reign was remarkable in other ways. The Industrial Revolution transformed Great Britain from a farm society into an industrial society, doubling its population. The country also added many new colonies, defeated the French dictator Napoleon after several wars, and had a tremendous flowering in the arts.

Geronimo
Apache Warrior
1829-1909

WHAT WOULD I YELL IF I JUMPED OUT OF A PLANE?

George Gershwin & Ira Gershwin
(1898-1937)   (1896-1983)
Jazz Songwriters

The Gershwin brothers—George and Ira—from Brooklyn, New York, became one of the hottest songwriting teams in the early 20th century. George composed the music; Ira wrote the words. Together, they penned such hit songs as "I Got Rhythm" and "Swanee," and wrote the scores to several Hollywood movies and Broadway musicals.

Their play *Of Thee I Sing* won the Pulitzer Prize in 1932, the first time a musical comedy had done so. George wrote the music for *Porgy and Bess*, the most popular American opera ever written, while Ira wrote the lyrics (words). George also wrote "Rhapsody in Blue," an enduring orchestral classic.

Geronimo was a feared warrior of the Chiricahua Apache, who lived in the Southwest U.S. and northern Mexico. Born Goyaale, which means "the smart one," Geronimo began raiding settlers in the U.S. and Mexico after his own family was killed in 1858.

Geronimo and his small band of followers escaped from reservations twice. They made bloody raids before finally being rounded up for good in 1885. He was eventually sent to Fort Sill, Oklahoma, where he became a successful farmer and a well-known celebrity. In 1906, Geronimo published an autobiography, *Geronimo's Story of His Life*.

Althea Gibson
Tennis Star
1927-

On August 25, 1950, Althea Gibson became the first black tennis player to play in the tournament now known as the U.S. Open. A year later she became the first black American to play at Wimbledon in England. Gibson's participation in those tournaments destroyed the color barrier that had so long kept black Americans out of professional tennis.

In 1957, Gibson took her accomplishments a step further: She won the singles titles in the U.S. Open as well as Wimbledon, the first black woman to do so. A year later, she repeated her success at both tournaments.

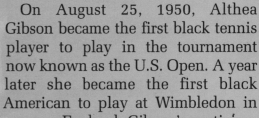

John Glenn
Pioneering Astronaut
1921-

John Glenn made history on February 20, 1962, in his space capsule *Friendship 7*, when he became the first American to orbit Earth. At the time, the U.S. space program trailed the Soviet Union's. Glenn's success gave the U.S. space program a much-needed boost, and he was honored with parades and medals.

Before becoming an astronaut, Glenn was a decorated fighter pilot who flew 149 missions during World War II and the Korean War. He later became a U.S. senator from Ohio; in 1984, he ran unsuccessfully for president. In October 1998, at age 77, Glenn flew on the space shuttle *Discovery*, becoming the oldest person to visit space.

Robert H. Goddard
Father of Modern Rocketry
1882-1945

At age 17, Robert Goddard became interested in rockets after reading *The War of the Worlds*, a science-fiction novel by H. G. Wells. Goddard, who wanted to build an engine that could be used for space flight, spent the rest of his life making the rocket practical.

Goddard launched the first flight of a liquid-fueled rocket in 1926. In 1935, he launched the first liquid-fueled rocket that could go faster than the speed of sound. Much of Goddard's work was scoffed at or ignored while he was alive, but soon after his death people began to recognize his amazing contributions to rocketry.

Samuel Gompers
Labor Leader
1850-1924

In 1886, American labor unions were mostly weak and ineffective. Samuel Gompers not only made his own union of cigar-makers stronger; he also folded a number of unions into a larger organization called the American Federation of Labor (AFL). Within six years, the AFL represented one million U.S. workers in a variety of fields.

Many labor groups had tried to make sweeping political changes, almost always without success. Gompers focused instead on getting higher wages from employers. He also looked for specific ways to help workers, such as getting laws passed that would abolish child labor. In 1955, the AFL combined with the Congress of Industrial Organizations (CIO) to become the AFL-CIO.

Jane Goodall
Zoologist
1934-

Jane Goodall is the world's leading authority on chimpanzees. As a young woman in the 1960s, she went to Africa and has spent most of her life there, studying animals in their natural habitat and trying to protect them. Goodall has also written books on chimpanzees, including *My Life With the Chimpanzees*, *The Chimpanzee Family Book*, and *In the Shadow of Man*.

Goodall lives closely with the chimpanzees she studies, and has made some surprising discoveries. For instance, she discovered that chimpanzees are the only animals other than humans that make and use tools. She also found that chimpanzees, like humans, sometimes kill each other for no apparent reason.

Mikhail Gorbachev
Last Leader of the Soviet Union
1931-

When Mikhail Gorbachev *(gawr-buh-CHAWF)* became president of the Soviet Union in 1985, he tried to reform its troubled communist system. His political and economic reforms were called *perestroika (PER-uh-STROY-kuh)*, which means "restructuring." *Glasnost (GLAZ-nosh)*, which means "openness," was his call for social freedoms.

Gorbachev's reforms encouraged European communist countries to overthrow their dictators in 1989. Gorbachev could have used force to stop these revolutions, but he refused. As a result, he won the 1990 Nobel Peace Prize.

In 1991, hard-line communists overthrew Gorbachev in an effort to reverse his reforms. However, their takeover was crushed by democratic forces. The Soviet Union broke up into different countries, and Gorbachev was forced out of office.

Francisco de Goya
Painter
1746-1828

The Spaniard Francisco de Goya is considered by many art historians to be the first modern artist. His work differed from that of other artists because he showed daily life, poked fun at powerful figures, and expressed his rage at human folly. His free-spirited painting style influenced many later artists.

In 1792, Goya became deaf, causing him to become isolated. His paintings grew more brooding, yet more powerful. Spain's war against France from 1808 to 1813 inspired some of his greatest works, which show the harshness of war. In 1824, he was forced to flee from Spain to France, because Spain's new king disapproved of his work.

Martha Graham
Pioneer of Modern Dance
1894-1991

Martha Graham helped change the face of modern dance. During her 70-year career, she created 180 dance works and frequently performed in the lead role. Among her most famous works were *Appalachian Spring* and *Acrobats of God*.

Graham's dances differed greatly from traditional ballet. She used her body to express complicated emotions, even if doing so required unpredictable or ungraceful moves.

After she retired from the stage in 1969, Graham continued to teach and choreograph dances. Many of the world's greatest dancers studied with her. Graham was an exacting teacher, but her skill commanded great respect.

Wayne Gretzky
Hockey Superstar
1961-

Ulysses S. Grant
Civil War General and 18th U.S. President
1822-1885

Ulysses S. Grant's life swung wildly between success and failure. Born Hiram Ulysses Grant, he graduated from West Point (where his name was changed) in 1843. His army career went nowhere. He left the army only to face failure as a businessman.

Success smiled on Grant when the Civil War broke out in 1861. He quickly became a Union officer; by 1864, he was supreme commander of the Union forces. His steady leadership guided the North to victory.

A national hero, Grant was elected president in 1868. However, his two terms in office were marred by corruption. Although Grant himself was honest, the scandals of people in his government caused him to be ranked a poor president.

Wayne Gretzky is probably the greatest ice hockey player to ever lace up skates. At 17, he became the youngest player in professional hockey. He went on to shatter almost every record in the National Hockey League (NHL).

He became the first player to score 200 points in a single season. He also holds single-season records in points (215), goals (92), and assists (163). In 1990, he became the first player to score 2,000 lifetime points. Gretzky led the Edmonton Oilers to the Stanley Cup championships in four of his eight seasons with that team. He also played with the Los Angeles Kings, St. Louis Blues, and New York Rangers.

Florence Griffith Joyner
Olympic Track Star
1959–1998

Florence Griffith Joyner was known for two things: her blazing speed on the track and her flamboyant way of dressing. "Flo Jo," as she was known, became an instant celebrity at the 1988 Seoul Olympics, after she set world records in the 100- and 200-meter dashes. In all, she won four gold medals that year.

The news media loved Griffith Joyner because she wore outrageous-looking outfits and extremely long, decorated fingernails. After retiring from sports in 1989, she pursued a career in television and designed sportswear. Griffith Joyner died unexpectedly of heart failure in 1998.

Jakob Grimm & Wilhelm Grimm
1785–1863   1786–1859
Storytellers

HAS ANY-ONE SEEN THE WOLF?

If you have ever heard such stories as "Hansel and Gretel," "Snow White," or "Little Red Riding Hood," you can thank the brothers Grimm. In the early 1800s, the inseparable brothers, who were German-language professors, collected folk stories told by poor German peasants, then published them in a book now known as *Grimms' Fairy Tales*.

The main goal of the Grimm brothers was to preserve the stories, but they also believed that the tales expressed German national pride. They retold most stories just as they heard them. However, they also edited many of them to suit current tastes or because they had heard several different versions of the same tale.

Johannes Gutenberg
Father of the Printing Press
1395–1468

Johannes Gutenberg *(yoh-HAHN-us GOOT-uhn-burg)* of Mainz, Germany, developed a process using movable type that allowed for quick and easy printing. A worker could print a page, then easily rearrange the letters to print a different page. This invention made it possible to mass-produce books and other printed matter for the first time, and set off an information revolution in Europe.

Chinese and Koreans invented movable type long before Gutenberg. However, their languages were so complex that movable type was not useful, and their inventions were forgotten.

Woody Guthrie
Folk Musician
1912-1967

During the Great Depression of the 1930s, Woody Guthrie became a musical voice for poor working people and the unemployed. He wrote more than 1,000 songs, the most famous of which was "This Land Is Your Land." Most were about ordinary people, or about Guthrie's ideas for social justice.

Woodrow Wilson Guthrie learned to play a guitar and harmonica as a teenager, and spent the 1930s living as a hobo. In 1937, he sang on a Los Angeles radio show, which made him famous. Guthrie spent his last 13 years plagued by a nerve disease. His work inspired many social activists as well as folk singers, including Bob Dylan.

Edmond Halley
Astronomer
1656-1742

Path of Halley's comet

Edmond Halley (HAL-ee) was one of England's greatest astronomers. While he was still a college student, he produced the first map of stars that are visible from the Southern Hemisphere. He also found an accurate way to measure the distance from the Earth to the sun.

However, Halley is best remembered for his study of comets. In his time, people believed that comets appeared by chance and could not be predicted. Halley recognized patterns in their appearance. He accurately predicted the 1758 return of a bright comet that had been seen in 1531, 1607, and 1682. Halley's comet, as it is now known, returns about every 76 years. It was last seen in 1986.

Fannie Lou Hamer
Civil-rights Activist
1917-1977

In the 1960s, Southern blacks were often required to take literacy tests in order to vote. This was designed to exclude them, because many blacks were permitted only little or very poor schooling.

Fannie Lou Hamer (HAY-mur) helped blacks to pass literacy tests and fought for their right to vote and observe other civil rights. As a result, she was thrown off her land in Mississippi and attacked by racists.

Hamer, the youngest of a sharecropper's 20 children, refused to be intimidated. She bravely fought racism all her life. Her most famous saying, "I'm sick and tired of being sick and tired," is engraved on her tombstone.

Alexander Hamilton
Founding Father
1757-1804

Alexander Hamilton, a gifted politician and writer, rose to prominence as a close aide to General George Washington during the American Revolution (1775-1783). After the war, Hamilton pushed for the U.S. to write a new constitution that created a strong central government. Once it was written in 1787, he was key in getting it approved by the 13 states.

Under President Washington, Hamilton became the first Secretary of the Treasury, and helped restore the country's financial health. Later, he became the leader of the Federalist Party, one of the first political parties in the U.S. Hamilton was killed in a duel with Aaron Burr, a former vice president who was Hamilton's political rival.

Hammurabi
Ancient Lawgiver
Unknown-1750 B.C.

Hammurabi (ham-oo-RAH-bee) was a king of ancient Babylon in the Middle East. An intelligent, careful ruler, he expanded his kingdom greatly during his 42-year reign. However, he is best remembered for a series of laws now known as the Code of Hammurabi—one of the first legal codes in history.

The main goal of the code was to protect the weak from the strong. It regulated everything from family life to criminal acts to trade and commerce. The laws seem harsh by modern standards, but they were reasonable compared to the unpredictable rule under which people had lived before.

W. C. HANDY
"FATHER OF THE BLUES"
1873-1958

W. C. Handy is the composer most responsible for making the blues popular in the early 1900s. The blues are a major form of American folk music, which sprang directly from African American tradition.

In 1909, William Christopher Handy wrote his first hit song, the "Memphis Blues." Though cheated out of the profits for that song, he went on to write other hits, including "St. Louis Blues."

As a young man, Handy toured the South as a musician, playing the cornet. As he traveled, he wrote down many of the blues songs that he heard from ordinary people. Handy later led his own band, started a music-publishing company, and promoted concerts.

I DID ALL THE WALKING!

Hannibal
Military Genius
247-183 B.C.

Hannibal was born into the ruling family of Carthage, a North African city that fought three bitter wars with ancient Rome between 264 B.C. and 146 B.C. Both Carthage and Rome had empires around the Mediterranean Sea, and each feared the other's power.

During the Second Punic War, Hannibal dealt Rome's armies some of their worst defeats ever. At one point, he could have captured and destroyed Rome. However, he hesitated; in the meantime, the Romans regrouped.

Over the next 14 years, the war turned against Hannibal, and Carthage was defeated. Hannibal managed to rebuild Carthage's power, but the Romans hunted him until he committed suicide.

Stephen Hawking
Scientist
1942–

Stephen Hawking is a widely admired physicist who has made several path-breaking discoveries about gravity. Hawking specializes in the study of black holes—collapsed giant stars that have a force of gravity so strong that not even light can escape them.

A Brief History of Time, Hawking's 1988 book, became a surprise hit and turned him into a celebrity outside the world of science. His achievements have been all the more remarkable because he suffers from Lou Gehrig's disease, a rare nervous-system disorder. Hawking uses a motorized wheelchair, and cannot speak without the help of machines.

William Randolph Hearst
Newspaper Publisher
1863-1951

I'M THE YELLOW KID!

In 1887, William Randolph Hearst's wealthy father gave him a failing San Francisco newspaper. Hearst turned it into a financial success by using sensational stories and screaming headlines. Hearst bought other big-city newspapers and ran them the same way. In 1898, their outrageous stories helped propel the U.S. into fighting the Spanish-American War.

Hearst pioneered the use of comic strips in newspapers. One of the first comic strips was called "The Yellow Kid." Because of that strip, the often-unethical style of reporting that Hearst encouraged was called "yellow journalism."

Hearst's company is still a powerful force in publishing and broadcasting. The movie *Citizen Kane* is based on Hearst's life.

Ernest Hemingway
Novelist
1899-1961

Patrick Henry
Founding Father
1736-1799

Patrick Henry was an exciting and influential speaker in colonial America. In 1775, Henry rallied his native Virginia to the cause of the American Revolution with a ringing speech that ended with these now-famous words: "I know not what course others may take, but as for me, give me liberty, or give me death."

Henry served as Virginia's governor four times. After the war, he opposed the U.S. Constitution because he feared that it would trample on the rights of individuals and of states. However, he later embraced it. He became a major force in the campaign to adopt the Bill of Rights—the first 10 amendments to the Constitution.

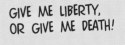

GIVE ME LIBERTY, OR GIVE ME DEATH!

Ernest Hemingway was one of the most famous writers of the 20th century. He developed a clear, concise writing style that has been widely imitated. He also had a thirst for adventure that led him all over the world, reporting on wars, watching Spanish bullfights, and going on African safaris.

Hemingway drew on his life experiences for his writing. For many readers, his exploits defined manliness. His greatest works include *A Farewell to Arms*, *For Whom the Bell Tolls*, and *The Old Man and the Sea*. Hemingway won the Pulitzer Prize in 1953 and the Nobel Prize in 1954.

Henry VIII
King of England
1491-1547

Henry VIII, the burly ruler of Renaissance England, is best known for having had six wives. Henry's desire to marry Anne Boleyn, his second, led to a fight with the Roman Catholic Church. In 1534, Henry broke off England's ties with the Catholic pope and made England a Protestant country.

Henry began as a reformer, but ended up a selfish, cruel ruler. He often killed people who opposed him—or people he *thought* were opposing him. However, he also built up the country's navy and helped make England a world power. Henry's use of political power at home was brilliant, and he remained popular with ordinary people throughout his life.

Jim Henson
Muppets Creator
1936-1990

Without Jim Henson, there would be no Kermit the Frog, Miss Piggy, Big Bird, Bert and Ernie, or Oscar the Grouch. In 1954, he created the first Muppets, a cross between marionettes and hand-held puppets. Henson was also the voice for Kermit the Frog and several other Muppet characters.

The Muppets became nationally famous in 1969, when they began appearing on *Sesame Street*, an educational children's show. From 1976 to 1981, Henson produced *The Muppet Show*, which was seen in more than 100 countries. The Muppets also starred in movies, including *The Muppet Movie*, *The Great Muppet Caper*, *The Muppets Take Manhattan*, and *Muppets From Space*.

Edmund Hillary
First to Reach
Mount Everest's Peak
1919-

On May 29, 1953, mountain climber Edmund Hillary of New Zealand and his guide, Tenzing Norgay of Nepal, became the first people to reach the top of Mount Everest. At 29,028 feet high, Everest is the tallest mountain on Earth. For that accomplishment, Hillary was knighted by Great Britain's Queen Elizabeth.

In later years, Hillary climbed other high mountains. He also led a search for the Abominable Snowman, but—like many other searches—found no reliable evidence that it exists. Hillary wrote a book, *High Adventure*, about his Everest climb.

Herodotus
Father of
History Writing
484-425

Herodotus *(hih-RAHD-uh-tus)* is widely credited with inventing history writing. Earlier writers had recorded past events, but they did so to glorify a king, praise an ancestor, or pass on a religion. Herodotus was the first writer whose main goal was to simply write down what he had learned.

Herodotus was a Greek who traveled widely and wrote mainly about Greece's wars with Persia in the early 5th century B.C. Many of the stories that he recounted sound far-fetched, and even he doubted their accuracy. However, archaeologists and later historians have shown many of them to be at least partially true.

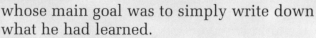

Hippocrates
Early Physician
460-377 B.C.

Hippocrates *(hih-PAHK-ruh-teez)* is often called the Father of Medicine, but we know very little about him. In ancient Greece, he was considered the greatest of doctors. At that time, people blamed supernatural causes for disease and illness. Hippocrates instead looked for natural causes, just as modern doctors do, then looked for appropriate cures. That was a tremendous advance in medicine.

Many writings long believed to have been written by Hippocrates were not, in fact, his works. That includes the famous Hippocratic oath, a statement of medical ethics that today's doctors recite upon graduation from medical school. However, Hippocrates is still honored for his groundbreaking work.

Hirohito
Emperor of Japan
1901~1989

Hirohito *(HEER-oh-HEE-toh)* was Japan's emperor during World War II (1939-1945). Hirohito disapproved of Japan's aggression before and during that war, but did little to stop it. Ordinary Japanese considered him to be a divine being (a god), but he had little real power. Near the war's end, however, he took action to stop further bloodshed by surrendering when others wanted to keep fighting.

After the war, many Americans wanted Hirohito to be tried as a war criminal, along with other top Japanese officials. However, the emperor was considered so important to Japanese society that the U.S. allowed him to live out his rule. Hirohito lost his divine status and became merely a "symbol of the state."

ALFRED HITCHCOCK
MOVIE DIRECTOR
1899-1980

Film director Alfred Hitchcock was considered the master of suspense and horror in 20th-century cinema. Although his movies were sometimes scary, they relied more on psychological terror than violence and gore.

Born in England, Hitchcock started as a director there. In 1939, he moved to the U.S. He is best remembered for his later movies. Among his hits were *Rebecca*, *Spellbound*, *Rear Window*, and *North By Northwest*.

Two Hitchcock movies in particular—*The Birds* and *Psycho*—are considered pioneering horror movies. *Rebecca* won an Academy Award for best picture, but Hitchcock never won the award for best director.

YOU MUST BE "PSYCHO" TO STAY HERE AT THE BATES MOTEL!

Adolf Hitler
German Dictator
1889-1945

Adolf Hitler was responsible for more terror and death than anyone in modern history, other than Josph Stalin. Hitler had powerful speaking skills and was able to turn followers into fanatics. He and his Nazi Party used those tools to capture power in Germany in 1933.

Hungry for conquests, Hitler started World War II in 1939. For three years he ruled most of Europe. Hitler's racist ideas led to the massacre of six million Jews as well as millions of Gypsies, Slavs, and other civilians. By 1945, the U.S., Great Britain, and the Soviet Union had defeated Hitler's armies. The Nazi dictator killed himself to avoid capture.

Ho Chi Minh
Vietnamese Nationalist
1890-1969

In the early 1900s, the country of Vietnam was a colony of France. During the 1930s, Ho Chi Minh *(hoh chee min)* became the leading voice for independence from France's harsh rule. Ho, a communist, told the French: "You can kill ten of my men for every one I kill of yours. But even at those odds, you will lose and I will win."

Declaring Vietnam's independence in 1945, Ho's forces finally defeated the French in 1954. Vietnam was divided into North Vietnam, with Ho as its president, and noncommunist South Vietnam. Ho sought to reunify his country. The result was the Vietnam War (1955-1975), in which U.S. troops fought from 1964 until 1975. When U.S. troops withdrew, South Vietnam surrendered.

Billie Holiday
Jazz and Blues Singer
1915-1959

When Billie Holiday sang the blues, she could move a roomful of listeners to tears with her distinctive style and singing voice. Her own childhood was sadder than any song she ever sang. Born Eleanora Fagan in Baltimore, she lived in poverty and endured terrible abuse as a child.

Holiday (who took the names Billie from her favorite actor, Billie Dove, and Holiday from her father) began her singing career in New York night clubs in 1931. By 1937, she was touring with such big-name musicians as Count Basie. As her success grew, though, "Lady Day" (as she was known) turned to drugs and other self-destructive behavior. By the 1950s, her voice had given out. She died at age 44 as a result of her drug abuse.

Oliver Wendell Holmes Jr.
Supreme Court Justice
1841-1935

Oliver Wendell Holmes Jr. is one of the most famous justices to sit on the U.S. Supreme Court. Whenever the high court hands down a majority opinion, the minority of justices who disagree with it can publish a *dissent*. Holmes became known as "the Great Dissenter" because he disagreed with the court's conservative majority so often.

Holmes, named to the bench in 1902 by President Theodore Roosevelt, served for 30 years. In time, his opinions about allowing unpopular speech and supporting organized labor later became majority views on the Supreme Court.

Homer
Poet of Ancient Greece
[dates unknown]

Homer is known as the author of two of the world's most famous epic poems, the *Iliad* and the *Odyssey*. However, very little is known about him. In fact, no one is sure that he really existed! Even the legendary information that we have about him is scanty. Homer is said to have been a blind poet who recited his poems. (They were not written down until many years later.) Several cities claimed to be his birthplace and burial place.

Many scholars today believe that Homer's masterpieces were the work of at least two poets who lived around 800 to 700 B.C. Regardless, the *Iliad* and the *Odyssey* are Europe's first great literary works. They were the foundation for Greek civilization, which, in turn, forms the foundation of modern civilization.

Harry Houdini
Magician and Escape Artist
1874-1926

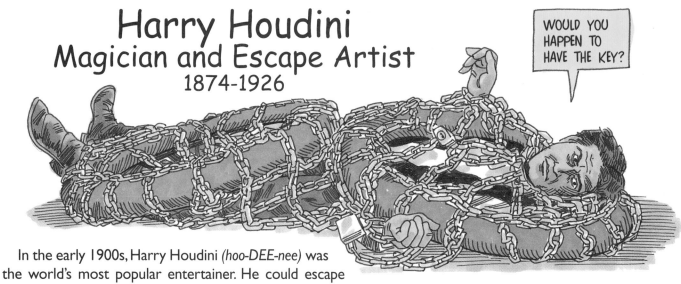

WOULD YOU HAPPEN TO HAVE THE KEY?

In the early 1900s, Harry Houdini (hoo-DEE-nee) was the world's most popular entertainer. He could escape from anything—handcuffs, straitjackets, jail cells, or water tanks. He even escaped from a locked box that had been thrown into a river! Houdini earned his fame by doing live shows, but also appeared in several movies.

Born Erich Weiss in Hungary, Houdini was the son of a Jewish rabbi. His family immigrated to the U.S. Young Erich worked hard to master escape skills. In later life, Houdini used his knowledge to expose frauds who claimed that they could read minds or speak with the dead. He was able to show that they used tricks, not magical powers, to cheat their customers.

Sam Houston
Statesman
1793-1863

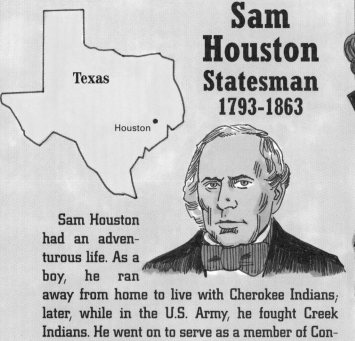

Texas

Houston

Sam Houston had an adventurous life. As a boy, he ran away from home to live with Cherokee Indians; later, while in the U.S. Army, he fought Creek Indians. He went on to serve as a member of Congress, then as governor of Tennessee.

In 1836, Houston became military leader of American settlers who wanted Texas to win independence from Mexico. His small army scored a decisive victory at the Battle of San Jacinto; he soon became the first president of the Republic of Texas. In 1845, Houston helped Texas become the 28th state in the Union, and served as its governor. The Texas city of Houston was named in his honor.

Elias Howe
Inventor of the Sewing Machine
1819-1867

Before Elias Howe invented the sewing machine, the fastest that a person could sew was about 50 stitches per minute—and it was exhausting work. Howe's machine, which could crank out 250 stitches per minute, made the job much faster and easier.

In 1846, Howe got a patent for his invention, which gave him exclusive legal rights to it. However, many sneaky manufacturers sold sewing machines but kept all the money. In 1854, after a long legal fight, Howe established his right to be paid. Howe was finally able to collect the money owed to him for every sewing machine sold.

Edwin Hubble
Astronomer
1889-1953

Edwin Hubble made two major discoveries in the field of astronomy during the 1920s. Back then, astronomers could not agree whether some parts of the nighttime sky were independent galaxies or if they belonged to our galaxy, the Milky Way. In 1924, Hubble proved that they were independent galaxies.

In 1929, Hubble made his greatest discovery. He showed that those other galaxies were moving away from us, proving that the universe is still expanding. That discovery had a tremendous impact on theories about the origin of life. The Hubble Space Telescope, a giant reflecting telescope that orbits Earth, is named after Hubble.

Langston Hughes
Writer
1902-1967

Langston Hughes was a prolific writer who turned out fine plays, essays, short stories, and novels. However, he is best remembered for his poetry, which combined traditional poetic forms with the rhythms of popular jazz music.

Hughes' poetry, like all his writing, reflects the pride that African Americans felt in the early 1900s, despite their status as second-class citizens. During the 1920s, black culture flowered in New York's Harlem neighborhood, and Hughes became a leader in this "Harlem Renaissance."

Besides his poetry, Hughes's most popular writings were short sketches that involved a character named Simple, who represented ordinary blacks. Simple often expressed his views in an amusing way.

David Hume
Philosopher
1711-1776

David Hume was one of the greatest philosophers of the Enlightenment. The Enlightenment is the name that historians gave to a period during the 1600s and 1700s when many people began to question old ideas of political and religious authority.

Hume believed that all human knowledge comes from experience rather than from ideas pre-formed in our minds. He also argued against many religious ideas, such as miracles.

Hume's writings angered religious authorities and kept him from becoming a professor at any Scottish university. Nevertheless, he remains one of the most important influences on modern philosophy.

Anne Hutchinson
Puritan Leader
1591-1643

Anne Hutchinson was a devout Puritan who lived in the Massachusetts Bay colony. However, her beliefs were different from those of the colony's leaders. For instance, she believed that God spoke to people directly, not through church leaders. She held meetings in her home to spread her beliefs.

In 1637, the church's leaders forced Hutchinson and her family to leave Massachusetts and flee to the neighboring colony of Rhode Island. A number of people who shared Hutchinson's ideas went with them. Later, she moved to New York, where she and most of her family were killed by Indians. Her outspokenness helped to establish the principle of religious freedom in the 13 colonies.

Lee Iacocca
Automobile Executive
1924-

Lee Iacocca *(EYE-uh-KOH-kuh)* has had a roller-coaster career as a leader in the automobile industry. In the late 1960s, as an executive at the Ford Motor Company, he pushed for the creation of the Ford Mustang. It became one of the best-selling car models ever.

In the 1970s, Iacocca was president of Ford when the company produced the Ford Pinto. Ford engineers knew that the car was unsafe, but the company produced it, anyway. Hundreds of people were killed, which tarnished the company's image.

In 1980, Lee Iacocca became president of the Chrysler Corporation, a carmaking company that was about to go bankrupt. Within four years, however, Iacocca turned the company's financial fortunes around, and became a national celebrity.

Henrik Ibsen
Playwright
1828-1906

Henrik Ibsen is considered the father of modern playwriting. When Ibsen began his career, theater in Europe and the U.S. had become shallow and superficial. Most plays contained unbelievable dialogue and relied on silly coincidences to keep an audience's attention. Ibsen helped turn things around by creating realistic characters who faced real-life problems.

Ibsen's first successful play was *The Warrior's Barrow* in 1850. Some of his most famous plays include *A Doll's House*, *Ghosts*, and *An Enemy of the People*. Ibsen's works are still frequently performed, and they have been translated into dozens of languages.

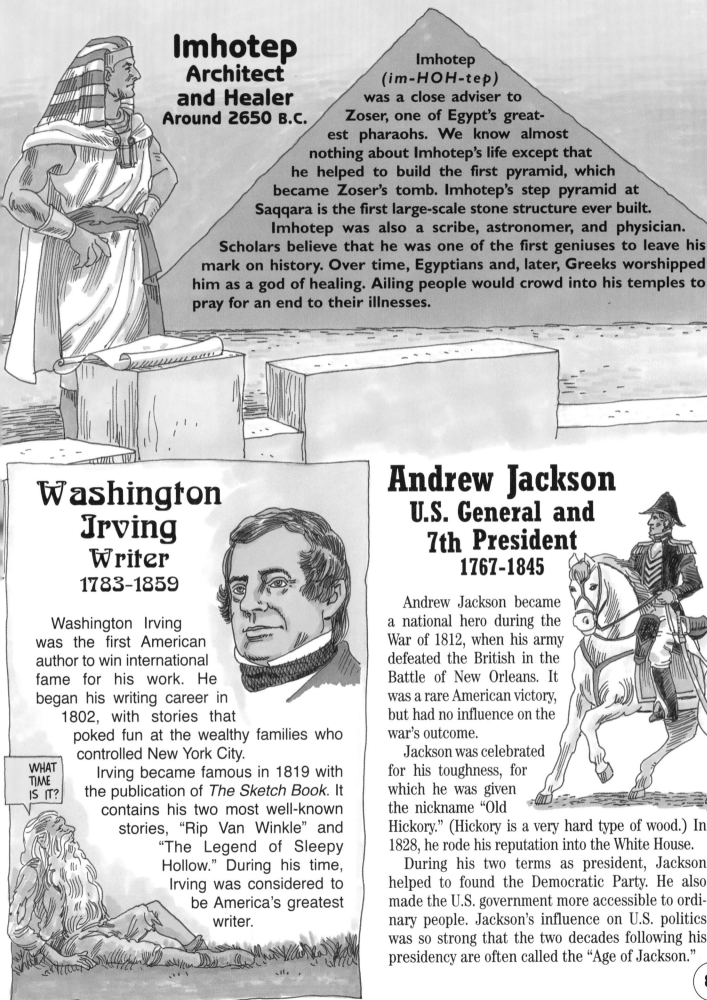

Imhotep
Architect and Healer
Around 2650 B.C.

Imhotep (im-HOH-tep) was a close adviser to Zoser, one of Egypt's greatest pharaohs. We know almost nothing about Imhotep's life except that he helped to build the first pyramid, which became Zoser's tomb. Imhotep's step pyramid at Saqqara is the first large-scale stone structure ever built. Imhotep was also a scribe, astronomer, and physician. Scholars believe that he was one of the first geniuses to leave his mark on history. Over time, Egyptians and, later, Greeks worshipped him as a god of healing. Ailing people would crowd into his temples to pray for an end to their illnesses.

Washington Irving
Writer
1783-1859

Washington Irving was the first American author to win international fame for his work. He began his writing career in 1802, with stories that poked fun at the wealthy families who controlled New York City.

Irving became famous in 1819 with the publication of *The Sketch Book*. It contains his two most well-known stories, "Rip Van Winkle" and "The Legend of Sleepy Hollow." During his time, Irving was considered to be America's greatest writer.

WHAT TIME IS IT?

Andrew Jackson
U.S. General and 7th President
1767-1845

Andrew Jackson became a national hero during the War of 1812, when his army defeated the British in the Battle of New Orleans. It was a rare American victory, but had no influence on the war's outcome.

Jackson was celebrated for his toughness, for which he was given the nickname "Old Hickory." (Hickory is a very hard type of wood.) In 1828, he rode his reputation into the White House.

During his two terms as president, Jackson helped to found the Democratic Party. He also made the U.S. government more accessible to ordinary people. Jackson's influence on U.S. politics was so strong that the two decades following his presidency are often called the "Age of Jackson."

Jesse Jackson
Civil-rights Leader
1941-

The son of a poor South Carolina family, Jesse Jackson was ordained a Baptist minister in 1968. While still in school, he became involved in the struggle to improve civil rights and economic opportunities for black Americans. Since the assassination of Martin Luther King Jr. in 1968, Jackson has become the most prominent African American in U.S. politics.

In 1984 and 1988, Jackson campaigned to become the Democratic nominee for president. Both attempts were unsuccessful. However, Jackson was the first African American to win strong support while making a serious run at the White House. His eloquent speeches call attention to the plight of less fortunate Americans of all races.

MICHAEL JACKSON
ROCK SUPERSTAR
1958-

Michael Jackson has been performing since he was five years old. In the 1960s, he and four older brothers formed the Jackson Five, with Michael as lead singer. The group had several number-one hits, including "I'll Be There" and "ABC."

The Jackson Five slumped during the early 1970s, and Michael began a solo career. In 1982, he released *Thriller*, which soon became the best-selling album of all time. In 1997, the Jackson Five were inducted into the Rock and Roll Hall of Fame. Aside from his music, Jackson is known for wearing unusual outfits (including just one silver glove) and for his distinctive "moonwalk" dancing.

JESSE JAMES
WESTERN OUTLAW
1847-1882

In Kansas during the U.S. Civil War, 15-year-old Jesse James joined Quantrill's raiders, a band of Confederate guerrillas (fighters who launch surprise attacks). The raiders killed pro-Union families and robbed mail coaches.

After the war, Jesse, his brother Frank, and several other Quantrill men began robbing banks and trains in the Midwest. Some historians have claimed that Jesse James often stole from the rich and gave to the poor. There is little evidence that James gave away money. However, there is a great deal of evidence that he was a cold-blooded killer. Jesse James was eventually betrayed and murdered by one of his own men.

John Jay
Founding Father
1745-1829

When the American Revolution first broke out, John Jay was opposed to it. However, he soon changed his mind and supported independence. He served in the Continental Congress and as a diplomat. Jay helped negotiate the treaty that ended the war.

After the war, Jay promoted efforts to create a strong central government. In 1789, he was named the first-ever chief justice of the U.S. Supreme Court. In 1794, John Jay negotiated a treaty with Great Britain that settled several problems left over from the American Revolution. The Jay Treaty helped smooth over tensions between the U.S. and Great Britain.

Thomas Jefferson
Founding Father and 3rd U.S. President
1743-1826

If Thomas Jefferson had done nothing after writing the Declaration of Independence in 1776, he still would be considered a great man. (That document has become the guiding light for freedom-seeking people all over the world.) Yet he went on to become the first secretary of state, the second vice president, and the third president of the U.S. He contributed greatly to the new country's stability by making the Louisiana Purchase, which doubled the U.S. in size, and waging war against pirates in Tripoli (now part of Libya, in northern Africa).

After leaving the White House, Jefferson returned to his native Virginia, where he founded the University of Virginia in Charlottesville, near his home, Monticello. Jefferson was also a talented architect, inventor, musician, philosopher, and farmer—one of the most remarkable men to live in the White House.

Edward Jenner
Discoverer of the Smallpox Vaccine
1749-1823

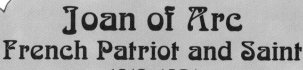

OUCH!

HOLD STILL!

Smallpox was one the deadliest diseases in history. In the 1700s, the only people safe from it were those who had caught it and survived. Edward Jenner, an English doctor, heard that dairymaids who caught cowpox from working with cows did not catch smallpox. Cowpox is similar to smallpox, but much milder. In 1796, he decided to try an experiment.

Jenner deliberately gave cowpox to a healthy boy. After the boy recovered, Jenner gave him what would normally be a deadly dose of smallpox. The boy did not get sick! The cowpox had made him *immune* to smallpox—that is, made his body build defenses against it. Jenner had discovered the world's first vaccine. About two centuries later, smallpox disappeared.

Joan of Arc
French Patriot and Saint
1412-1431

When Joan of Arc was born, France and England had been fighting on French soil for nearly 100 years. Joan, a peasant girl who saw heavenly visions, believed that she could help the French get rid of the English. With great difficulty, she convinced France's desperate king to let her lead an army.

Joan surprised everyone by winning several smashing victories. Then she was captured in battle by the English. Joan was tried as a witch and burned at the stake. A later court reversed the charge of witchcraft. In 1920, the Roman Catholic church proclaimed her a saint.

Steven Jobs & Steven Wozniak
1955–   1950–
Founders of Apple Computer

In the early 1970s, computers were massive, room-sized machines that only big companies and governments could afford. In 1976, two friends from California—Steven Jobs and Steven Wozniak—started a company called Apple Computers. They built the first small, personal computers to appeal to ordinary people.

Wozniak designed the computers; Jobs supplied the marketing know-how to sell them. By the early 1980s, Apple was a multibillion dollar company. The company and its founders have experienced ups and downs, and Apple's influence declined as other companies began to produce personal computers and related products. Nevertheless, Apple was a major force in starting the home-computer revolution.

APPLE COMPUTER

The original Apple computer →

Jack Johnson
First Black Heavyweight Champion
1878-1946

Jack Johnson was the first African American to win a heavyweight boxing championship. He did so in 1908, a time when most blacks in America faced brutal discrimination. Johnson became a hero to many. However, he was despised by white racists, who tried to find a "Great White Hope" to defeat him.

That proved difficult, because Johnson demolished every white challenger he faced. Finally, Johnson's enemies brought trumped-up legal charges against him. In 1915, Johnson lost his title to Jess Willard in a suspicious-looking fight. Many people believed that Johnson had lost deliberately, in hopes of getting the legal charges dropped. They were not. In 1920, Johnson was sent to a Kansas prison, where he served a one-year sentence.

Lyndon B. Johnson
36th U.S. President
1908-1973

On November 22, 1963, President John F. Kennedy was assassinated and Vice President Lyndon B. Johnson was sworn in to replace him. Johnson reassured Americans after the tragedy. He went on to become an impressive president, elected in his own right in 1964. LBJ, as he was called, was a born politician who loved high office. As part of his "Great Society" programs, he helped create landmark laws that supported civil rights, aid to the poor, health insurance, and education.

However, Johnson was dogged by the war in Vietnam. Johnson felt that he could not pull U.S. troops out of the fighting, yet public protests against the war kept growing. Finally, Johnson backed out of the 1968 presidential race.

Bobby Jones
Golf Legend
1902-1971

Bobby Jones was one of the greatest golfers to play the game. In 1930, he became the first player ever to win all of the four major golf tournaments in one year. From 1923 to 1930, he won 13 championships. That record stood until Jack Nicklaus broke it in 1973.

Robert Tyre Jones Jr. remained an amateur player throughout his career. After he retired, he helped found the Augusta National Golf Club in Augusta, Georgia. He also helped to establish the prestigious Masters tournament, still played there.

John Paul Jones
Hero of the American Revolution
1747-1792

John Paul Jones is the first naval hero in U.S. history, and he is considered the father of the U.S. Navy. His reputation was made in a sea battle he fought against the British on September 23, 1779, during the American Revolution.

Jones's ship, the *Bonhomme Richard*, attacked a much larger British ship, the *Serapis*. The two ships dueled for hours, and Jones's ship was badly damaged. Yet, when the British captain called on him to surrender, Jones made his now-famous reply: "I have not yet begun to fight!" Jones finally won the battle. Two days later, the *Bonhomme Richard* sank. Jones continued his journey on the captured *Serapis*.

Mother Jones
Labor Activist
1830-1930

When Mary Harris Jones was 37, she lost her husband and all four children in a yellow fever epidemic. Four years later, she lost her home and seamstress business in the great Chicago fire of 1871. After that, Jones dedicated herself to improving the lives of ordinary workers through organized labor. Workers affectionately called her "Mother Jones."

She focused much of her energy on helping to improve working conditions for coal miners and on ending child labor. Jones inspired people with her will to fight and sacrifice. During one speech, when she was 80 years old, she told the crowd, "There is going to be a racket and I am going to be in it!"

Scott Joplin
Ragtime Composer
1867 or 1868-1917

Around 1900, Scott Joplin's ragtime music—a lively combination of several folk styles—became very popular. Among his big hits were "Maple Leaf Rag" and "The Entertainer." Joplin became known as the King of Ragtime, although he was not the first or only musician to play that kind of music.

Joplin became obsessed with getting financial backing to stage a ragtime opera he had written, but failed. This disappointment, along with the effects of a long-term illness that eventually led to his early death, seems to have affected other creative work later in his life. For decades, Joplin's music was all but forgotten. However, it won new popularity in the 1970s, when his songs were used in *The Sting*, a hit movie.

Michael Jordan
Basketball Superstar
1963-

Michael Jordan is probably the greatest basketball player in the history of the game. In 1982, as a college freshman, he led the University of North Carolina to the national championship. He joined the Chicago Bulls of the National Basketball Association (NBA) for the 1984-1985 season, and was voted Rookie of the Year after scoring an average of 28.2 points a game—the third best in the league.

Jordan led the Bulls to an unprecedented six world championships, and the U.S. Olympic basketball team to two gold medals. His career scoring average of 31.5 points per game is the highest of any player in NBA history. Jordan became the most recognized athlete in the world during the 1990s.

Frida Kahlo
Painter
1907-1954

As a young woman, Frida Kahlo was badly injured in a bus accident. During her long recuperation, she learned how to paint. Most of her paintings were about personal subjects. They often reflected the physical pain that she felt all her life as a result of her injuries.

In 1929, Kahlo married Diego Rivera, a fellow Mexican artist. They had a stormy marriage. However, Rivera greatly influenced Kahlo's work. Some of her most famous paintings include *The Broken Column*, *Henry Ford Hospital*, and *The Birth of Moses*. Kahlo's fame as an artist has grown dramatically since her death.

Immanuel Kant
Philosopher
1724-1804

Immanuel Kant is considered one of the greatest of all modern philosophers (thinkers). He helped link two major schools of philosophical belief: rationalists and empiricists. *Rationalists* believe that knowledge comes from the mind. *Empiricists* believe that knowledge comes from experience. Kant also showed that God's existence cannot be proven or disproved by reason, as past philosophers had argued. He believed that there were other ways to prove that God exists.

Kant was a creature of habit. He never left his hometown of Königsberg, Germany, and his daily walk was so regular that neighbors set their clocks by it. He was a charming man who entertained frequently.

Helen Keller
Champion of the Deaf and Blind
1880-1968

A serious illness left Helen Keller blind and deaf when she was 18 months old. Cut off from communicating with others, Keller grew up wild and uncontrollable. When she was seven, her desperate parents hired a teacher named Annie Sullivan. Sullivan used the sense of touch to teach Keller the use of language. Once Keller discovered how to communicate in sign language, she learned quickly. She became an honors student, and went on to graduate from Radcliffe College in 1904. While still a student, she began writing her autobiography, *The Story of My Life*. It has been published in 50 languages.

Keller worked to improve conditions for the blind and the deaf, and became an international celebrity. The movie *The Miracle Worker* shows how Sullivan broke through to Keller's dark and soundless world.

John F. Kennedy
35th U.S. President
1917-1963

In 1960, John F. Kennedy became the youngest man to be elected U.S. president and the first Roman Catholic president. The youth and charm of Kennedy and his wife Jacqueline were widely admired. They often set fashion trends.

Kennedy's most serious crisis as president occurred in October 1962, when the Soviet Union placed nuclear weapons in Cuba, a small island country only 90 miles south of Florida. Kennedy demanded that the weapons be removed. The situation could have led to nuclear war but, after a tense standoff, the Soviets finally withdrew the weapons.

On November 22, 1963, Kennedy was assassinated in Dallas, Texas. His large extended family is still considered a kind of unofficial American royalty, and their activities are closely watched by the news media.

Jomo Kenyatta
Statesman
1893 or 1894-1978

AFRICA

KENYA

Jomo Kenyatta *(JOH-moh ken-YAH-tuh)* helped lead the East African country of Kenya to independence from Great Britain, won in 1963. He then served as Kenya's first prime minister. When Kenya became a republic a year later, he was elected president, a job that he held until his death.

As a boy, Kenyatta ran away from home to study at a Christian mission school. When he grew up, he began working with groups dedicated to ending British rule in Kenya. From 1953 to 1961, Kenyatta was imprisoned by the British, who accused him of promoting terrorism. Kenyatta denied the charge. During his presidency, Kenyatta worked to improve Kenya's economy and to smooth troubled race relations.

Johannes Kepler
Astronomer
1571–1630

Sun   Earth

Johannes Kepler *(yoh-HAHN-us KEP-lur)* was an important astronomer during the European Renaissance. The word *renaissance* means "rebirth"; Europe's Renaissance period was a time of rebirth in science, art, and learning.

In Kepler's time, scientists believed that planets moved in a circle around the sun. Using mathematical formulas, Kepler showed that they actually move in an ellipse (oval). This and other calculations helped later scientists explain how gravity works. Kepler made discoveries in optics as well. He helped to invent the astronomical telescope, and showed how lenses work. He also was the first person to correctly explain how light causes the eye to see objects.

JACK KEROUAC
WRITER
1922-1969

In the 1950s and early 1960s, many young Americans felt that they couldn't relate to mainstream culture in the U.S. They adopted unconventional lifestyles to escape it, and flocked to San Francisco, New York, and other big cities.

Jack Kerouac *(KEHR-oo-ak)* called these freewheeling people "the Beat generation." Through his novels and poems, he became their chief spokesperson. People who made this lifestyle choice became known as "beatniks." In 1957, Kerouac published his most famous novel, *On the Road*. It was a fictionalized account of Kerouac's aimless travels with friends around the country. In the late 1960s, the Beat movement that Kerouac championed evolved into the counterculture hippie movement.

Francis Scott Key
Author of "The Star-Spangled Banner"
1779-1843

In 1812, the U.S. and Great Britain went to war. Two years later, the War of 1812 was still raging. On September 13, 1814, the British shelled Baltimore's Fort McHenry. Francis Scott Key was on a ship in the harbor and had a ringside seat to the bombardment.

In the morning, Key could see that the fort had not surrendered—its flag was still flying. He excitedly wrote the words to "The Star-Spangled Banner." Key set the words to a British drinking song. Soon, it was widely sung as the national anthem. Congress did not officially recognize it as such until 1931.

Billie Jean King
Tennis Star
1943-

Billie Jean King was a standout tennis player in the 1960s and 1970s. She won many titles, especially at Wimbledon. She won the singles event there six times, the doubles ten times, and the mixed doubles four times. No one else has ever won so many Wimbledon titles.

In 1973, King played a widely publicized tennis match billed as "The Battle of the Sexes." Her opponent was Bobby Riggs, a male tennis star. Riggs had angered many people by making fun of women's tennis, which he claimed was inferior to men's. In that match, King defeated Riggs before an audience of 30,000 people in Houston's Astrodome. She continued to fight for equal pay and respect for female athletes in all sports.

Martin Luther King Jr.
Civil-rights Leader
1929-1968

Martin Luther King Jr. began his career as a minister at a small Baptist church in Montgomery, Alabama, but soon became famous nationwide as a civil-rights leader. In 1955 and 1956, he led nonviolent protests that helped desegregate Montgomery's buses. Over the next eight years, his efforts helped pass laws that banned discrimination (unequal treatment) based on race and gave blacks the right to vote.

On August 28, 1963, at a huge march for freedom and equal rights in Washington, D.C., King delivered his now-famous "I Have a Dream" speech. A year later, his nonviolent efforts for racial brotherhood won him a Nobel Peace Prize. He was assassinated in 1968. In 1983, Congress made the third Monday in January a national holiday in his honor.

Sandy Koufax
Baseball Star
1935-

Sandy Koufax was the premier left-handed pitcher in baseball during the 1960s. Playing for the Brooklyn Dodgers, Koufax won 165 games, lost 87, and compiled an earned run average of 2.76.

Koufax threw four no-hit games and twice led the Dodgers to the World Series. He was also voted the National League's most valuable player in 1963, and he won the Cy Young award three times. His 12-year career ended prematurely in 1966, when he developed arthritis in his left elbow. In 1972, at the age of 36, he became the youngest man ever elected to the National Baseball Hall of Fame.

Michelle Kwan
Figure Skater
1980-

Michelle Kwan began ice skating at age five, after seeing her brother play in an ice-hockey game. Then, after watching the 1988 Winter Olympics, she made up her mind to compete there herself.

Kwan has since become one of the top skaters in the world. She has won four national titles as well as a silver medal in the 1998 Winter Olympics. That same year, Kwan earned the highest number of perfect scores in the history of the United States Figure Skating Championships.

95

Marquis de Lafayette
(Marie Joseph Paul Yves Roch Gilbert du Motier)
Hero of the American Revolution
1757-1834

The Marquis de Lafayette was a French nobleman who fought with the colonial army during the American Revolution. (*Marquis* is a title of nobility, similar to *duke* or *earl*.) Lafayette served under General George Washington, and the two men became good friends. Lafayette, one of Washington's best officers, helped the American colonists get military aid from France.

After the war, Lafayette returned to France, where he played a key role in the French Revolution. When the king of France was overthrown in 1792, however, Lafayette was labeled a traitor. He barely escaped from France with his life. Two decades later, after Napoleon—France's emperor—was defeated at Waterloo, Lafayette once again became a strong force in French politics. He was warmly received when he returned to the U.S. in 1824.

Lao-tzu
Founder of the Taoist Religion
About 500 B.C.

Very little is known about Lao-tzu, the founder of Taoism. Along with Confucianism and Buddhism, Taoism is one of the three main religions of China.

According to legend, Lao-Tzu (which means "the Old Fellow" or "Grand Old Master" in Chinese) worked in the court of an emperor. He wrote down his teachings in a book called the *Tao-Te Ching*, or *The Classic of the Way of Power*.

A great deal of Taoist teaching relies on *paradox*—statements that seem to contradict each other. For instance, Taoism teaches that the greatest strength is weakness, and that happiness comes from disaster.

The Leakey Family
Discoverers of Early Humans

The Leakeys are leading figures in *paleontology* (the study of prehistoric times), and *anthropology* (the study of human cultures).

I'M PART OF THE FAMILY!

Louis Leakey (1903-1972) made several discoveries of ancient bones that reshaped our ideas about prehistoric times. He proved that humankind is far older than once believed. He also showed that the first humans came from Africa, not Asia, as scientists once thought. Leakey also was key in encouraging other scientists' work, such as Jane Goodall's study of chimpanzees and Dian Fossey's study of gorillas.

Mary Leakey (1913-1996)—wife of Louis and mother of Richard—was an accomplished scientist who made important discoveries on her own. In 1959, she discovered fossils in Africa that propelled her family to worldwide fame. In 1978, she made her greatest discovery: two pairs of footprints left by humanlike creatures who had been walking side by side. Although her husband was better known, many people regarded Mary Leakey as a more thorough scientist.

Richard Leakey (1944-) Though his parents were famous for their discoveries of early human bones and tools, as a young man Richard Leakey refused to follow in their footsteps. As he grew older, however, he realized that he liked fossil hunting, too. In 1972 and 1973, he made impressive finds of early human bones. In 1984, his team made one of the most spectacular discoveries in paleontology: the nearly complete skeleton of an early human boy. His wife Maeve and their daughter Louise are also paleontologists.

Robert E. Lee
Confederate General
1807-1870

Robert E. Lee was the Confederacy's most beloved and skillful general during the U.S. Civil War (1861-1865). Time after time, his cunning and boldness held back Union armies that were much larger than his own. Lee is widely considered one of the best military leaders in U.S. history.

Lee was born into a wealthy Virginia family, and distinguished himself early as a U.S. Army officer. After the Mexican War (1846-1848), he became superintendent of West Point. When his home state left the Union, he became an officer in the Confederate Army. Later, he was commander of all Confederate forces. When Lee finally surrendered in 1865, the Southern cause collapsed. After the war, Lee worked hard to promote peace and national unity.

Vladimir Lenin
Leader of the Russian Revolution
1870-1924

In October 1917, Vladimir Lenin led the revolution that turned Russia and neighboring countries into the Soviet Union, the world's first communist-ruled nation. Lenin was a follower of Karl Marx, a philosopher who opposed free enterprise and capitalism. Lenin wanted to set up a country in which the government controlled all businesses and farms.

Lenin—born Vladimir Ilich Ulyanov—used terror to win and keep power. People who opposed him were rounded up and imprisoned or killed. Free speech was banned. The Soviet Union continued those policies until its government was toppled in 1991. The communist system improved living conditions for many of its citizens, but it allowed little individual freedom.

Carl Lewis
Sprinter and Olympic Champion
1961-

For many years, Carl Lewis was the fastest man alive, setting several records in track and field. He won a total of nine gold medals at the Olympic Games of 1984, 1988, 1992, and 1996. He is only the second athlete to win a gold medal in the same event (the 4 x 100-meter relay) in four different Olympics.

At the 1988 games, Lewis placed second in the 100-meter dash. But when the winner tested positive for drug use and was disqualified, Lewis was awarded the gold medal.

Carl Lewis was inducted into the Olympic Hall of Fame in 1985. He retired from track in 1997.

Meriwether Lewis & William Clark
1774-1809   1770-1838
American Explorers

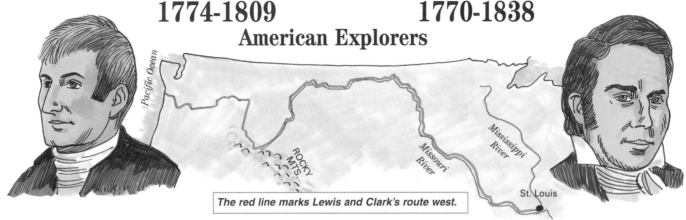

The red line marks Lewis and Clark's route west.

In the early 1800s, Americans knew very little about what lay west of the Mississippi River. President Thomas Jefferson asked Meriwether Lewis and William Clark to find out. In 1804, the pair set out with a team of about 50 explorers to learn about plants, animals, geography, and the Native American population.

One of Lewis and Clark's goals was to find a water route that could take settlers west. They did not find one. However, their "Corps of Discovery," as the team was called, reached the Pacific coast of Oregon. The team came back in 1806 with knowledge that paved the way for later explorers and settlers.

Sinclair Lewis
Novelist
1885–1951

In 1920, Sinclair Lewis's novel *Main Street* hit the U.S. like a cold slap in the face. It poked fun at the boring life that Lewis saw while growing up in small-town America, and many people were offended.

During the 1920s, Lewis wrote four other books: *Babbitt*, *Arrowsmith*, *Elmer Gantry*, and *Dodsworth*. Each book delighted some readers and annoyed others. *Elmer Gantry*, for instance, criticized leaders of organized religion. People in one Virginia town got so angry about it that they threatened to lynch Lewis.

Lewis turned down the Pulitzer Prize in 1924. But in 1930, he became the first American to win—and accept—the Nobel Prize for Literature.

Queen Liliuokalani
Queen of Hawaii
1838–1917

Queen Liliuokalani (*lee-LEE-uh-woh-kuh-LAHN-ee*) was the last monarch to reign over Hawaii before the islands were taken over by the U.S. She became queen in 1891, after the death of her brother, King David Kalakaua.

ALOHA!

The new queen soon tried to strengthen her power, but American businessmen—especially fruit growers—resisted her efforts. They finally overthrew Liliuokalani in 1893 and set up a republic that they controlled.

The queen made several unsuccessful attempts to get her throne back before the U.S. annexed Hawaii in 1898. Liliuokalani is also remembered for having written "Aloha Oe," Hawaii's farewell song.

Abraham Lincoln
16th U.S. President
1809-1865

Abraham Lincoln was born in a one-room log cabin in Kentucky and had very little formal schooling. He held many jobs before being elected to the Illinois legislature in 1834. Well before 1860, when the man known as "Honest Abe" became president, he had developed strong antislavery views.

Slavery, in large part, was dividing the North and South. Less than six weeks after he took office in 1861, the Civil War started. Though he wanted to preserve the Union, Lincoln made a bold decision: In 1863 he issued the Emancipation Proclamation, which freed slaves in Confederate states.

Lincoln eventually achieved his goal of preserving the Union. On April 9, 1865, just over a month after his second term in office began, the Civil War ended. Five days later, he was assassinated at Ford's Theater in Washington, D.C. He is remembered as one of the nation's greatest presidents.

Charles Lindbergh
First Pilot to Fly Solo Over the Atlantic
1902-1974

In 1927, American Charles Lindbergh became the first person to make a solo, nonstop flight over the Atlantic Ocean. The 3,600-mile flight from New York to Paris took him 33 1/2 hours to complete in his plane, the *Spirit of St. Louis*.

After the flight, Lindbergh—known as "Lucky Lindy" and the "Lone Eagle"—was showered with honors. Later, though, his reputation was tarnished when he fought to keep the U.S. out of World War II. He was even accused of being pro-Nazi. During the war, Lindbergh redeemed himself by flying 50 combat missions as a U.S. civilian. He also developed technology to help pilots.

CAROLUS LINNAEUS
NATURALIST
1707-1778

Carolus Linnaeus *(lin-nay-us)* invented the system that biologists now use to name plants and animals. It is called a *binomial* system, because it gives each plant or animal two Latin names. (*Bi-* means two; *nomial* comes from a Latin word meaning "name.") In Linnaeus's system, the first name identifies a plant or animal's genus, and the second name identifies its species. For example, a cougar is classified as a *Felis concolor*. Because of new scientific discoveries, the system has changed somewhat over time. However, scientists can still use it to identify any animal, no matter what language they speak.

Linnaeus was born Carl von Linné in Sweden. He became known by the Latin version of his name because he wrote in that language.

Joseph Lister
Pioneer of Cleanliness for Doctors
1827-1912

GIVE US GERMS A BREAK!

In the 1860s, when Joseph Lister was a surgeon in London, cutting a patient open for even the most minor surgery could lead to death. That was because doctors had few ways to stop infections, which could be fatal. Lister suspected that infections were caused by germs in the air and on surgeons' hands and tools. He began using antiseptics—chemicals that kill germs—as a sterilizer. Patient deaths fell dramatically.

At first, other doctors were hesitant to accept Lister's lifesaving methods. However, it soon became clear that he had made surgery much safer.

Belva Lockwood
Champion of Women's Rights
1830-1917

Belva Lockwood was almost 40 when she decided to study law. Even then, she was rejected from three law schools before National University in Washington, D.C., accepted her application in 1871.

At that time, there were very few female lawyers, and they were not allowed to argue before the U.S. Supreme Court. Lockwood pressured Congress to change the law, and eventually won. In 1879, she became the first woman to practice law before the high court. Later, she ran for president twice, as the candidate from the National Equal Rights Party.

Jack London
Novelist
1876-1916

During the early 1900s, U.S.-born John Griffith London—known as Jack—was one of the most popular novelists and journalists in the world. He grew up poor and had to work at a variety of jobs. In the 1890s, he joined the Alaskan gold rush, and that gave him material for many of his fictional works.

Two of London's best-known novels are *The Call of the Wild* and *White Fang*. His personal beliefs were sometimes odd. London hated capitalism and championed the cause of the poor. However, he also believed that whites were superior to other races. London's books remain well-read classics.

Louis XIV
King of France
1638-1715

I'M ALL DRESSED UP WITH NO PLACE TO GO!

Just four years old when he became king, Louis XIV ruled for 72 years—longer than any other European monarch. Louis, who chose the sun as his emblem, became known as the "Sun King."

Early in his reign, Louis chose good advisers, and France prospered in business and the arts. However, Louis—an absolute monarch—believed that he was above the law. "I am the state," he proclaimed.

Over time, wars and Louis's persecution of religious minorities greatly weakened France. The king's policies also deepened the poverty and resentment of ordinary French people and helped lead to the French Revolution of 1789.

Joe Louis
Heavyweight Boxing Champion
1914-1981

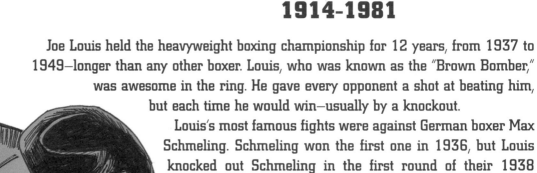

Joe Louis held the heavyweight boxing championship for 12 years, from 1937 to 1949—longer than any other boxer. Louis, who was known as the "Brown Bomber," was awesome in the ring. He gave every opponent a shot at beating him, but each time he would win—usually by a knockout.

Louis's most famous fights were against German boxer Max Schmeling. Schmeling won the first one in 1936, but Louis knocked out Schmeling in the first round of their 1938 rematch. The fights had political overtones because of Nazi Germany's racist policies, and because tensions were rising between the U.S. and Germany.

Auguste Lumière & Louis Jean Lumière
1862-1954   1864-1948
Movie and Photography Pioneers

In 1895, Auguste and Louis Jean Lumière *(loom-YAIR)* invented a movie camera that could both make movies and be used as a projector. Far better than any its competitors, it had components still used in projectors today, such as a claw movement that advances the film. Yet the brothers believed that their movie camera was an "an invention without a future."

Many of the earliest motion pictures were made using Lumière cameras. The Lumières were responsible for many other important advances in photography. In 1907, for instance, they invented the first practical color film.

Martin Luther
Leader of the Protestant Reformation
1483-1546

As a young man and devout Catholic, Martin Luther ignored his parents' wishes and became a monk. However, the corruption and worldliness that he saw among some Church officials bothered him. In 1517, Luther tried to debate these problems, which sparked a hostile reaction from the Church. His actions eventually led to the Reformation, a movement in which many Christians, known as Protestants, broke away from the Catholic Church. Luther, a German, translated the Bible into his native language. (Until then, all Bibles were written in Latin.) This allowed common people to read the Bible themselves for the first time, and greatly influenced the German language. Luther's legacy remains controversial, especially some of his writings that were hostile to Judaism. However, Luther is one of the most influential people in Christian history.

Douglas MacArthur
U.S. General
1880-1964

During World War II, Douglas MacArthur led U.S. Army forces in the Pacific. In 1942, the Japanese drove him from his base in the Philippines. "I shall return," he vowed, and did so two years later. MacArthur accepted Japan's surrender in 1945. He had great control over that country in the postwar years, and he reshaped Japanese government and society.

MacArthur also led U.S. military forces when the Korean War (1950-1953) broke out. However, President Harry S. Truman fired him for publicly questioning U.S. policy in Korea. MacArthur returned to the U.S. to a hero's welcome and retired from public life.

Niccolò Machiavelli
Renaissance Philosopher
1469-1527

Niccolò Machiavelli *(MAK-ee-uh-VEL-ee)* was the first true political scientist. He studied how to win power and keep it, and wrote his observations in an important book called *The Prince*. In *The Prince*, Machiavelli noted the many underhanded methods that leaders can use to achieve their goals. As a result, the word *Machiavellian* has come to mean "ruthless."

Machiavelli, an Italian politician and diplomat, was actually an ethical man who believed in representative government. However, he was also a realist. His writings reflected the sometimes-cruel world in which he lived—a world in which dictators believed that "the end justifies the means."

Dolley Madison
U.S. First Lady
1768-1849

In 1814, the U.S. was fighting the War of 1812 against Great Britain. That August, the British army invaded Washington, D.C., and burned down much of the city, including the White House. First Lady Dolley Madison, wife of President James Madison, escaped from the British just in time. She saved important state papers and a famous portrait of George Washington from the flames.

Madison was well known as a strong-minded woman with wit and charm. Long after her husband left office, she remained Washington's top hostess. As a sign of respect, she was given an honorary lifetime position in the House of Representatives.

James Madison
Founding Father and 4th U.S. President
1751-1836

James Madison is considered the Father of the U.S. Constitution. During the Constitutional Convention of 1787, his arguments greatly shaped the document. Once the convention reached agreement on the Constitution, Madison worked hard to get it approved by the 13 states. He also wrote the first 10 amendments to the Constitution, which are called the Bill of Rights.

In 1809-1817, Madison served as the fourth U.S. president. His two terms were marred by the War of 1812 (1812-1814). However, after the war, the U.S. began an "Era of Good Feeling" (1815-1825), a period during which political squabbling in Washington was minimized.

MADONNA ROCK STAR 1958–

Madonna hit it big as a solo rock singer in the early 1980s with her albums *Madonna* and *Like a Virgin*. She quickly became known for her unusual stage shows and her ability to keep changing her image. Fans loved her music and stage shows, and she emerged as one of the best-known women in the world in the late 1980s and early 1990s.

Madonna, who was born Madonna Louise Veronica Ciccone, used her musical success as a springboard for a movie career. Her attempts had mixed results. Two of her best-known movies are *Desperately Seeking Susan* and *Evita*. Both were popular with critics and audiences. Other films, however, did not fare as well.

Ferdinand Magellan
Portuguese Explorer
1480-1521

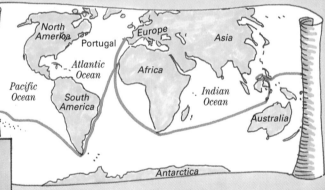

In 1519, Ferdinand Magellan (*muh-JEL-un*), a Portuguese sea captain, launched the first expedition to sail around the world. He was looking for a shortcut to islands in the Pacific now known as Indonesia, where valuable spices could be found. He never found it.

However, he did discover a waterway—now called the Strait of Magellan—at the tip of South America, and his crew became the first Europeans to cross the Pacific Ocean. Most expedition members died of the extreme hardships, and Magellan was killed in a fight with Philippine islanders. Only one of his five ships completed the voyage, returning to Spain in 1522.

Moses Maimonides
Jewish Philosopher
1135-1204

Moses Maimonides (*my-MAHN-uh-deez*) was the greatest Jewish philosopher of the Middle Ages. One of his main goals was to combine religious faith with reason as taught by ancient Greek philosophers. His work greatly influenced Jewish, Muslim, and Christian thinkers.

Maimonides was born in Córdoba, Spain, but his family had to flee from attacks by radical Muslims. Eventually, he settled in Egypt, where the Muslim sultan allowed other religions. Maimonides' fame as a doctor spread far and wide, and soon he became the personal physician to the sultan. He also became a leader in the Jewish community.

Malcolm X
Black Nationalist Leader
1925-1965

Malcolm X was one of the best-known and most radical leaders fighting for black Americans' rights in the 1960s. Born Malcolm Little, his childhood was wracked by racism, poverty, and crime. In 1946, he went to prison for burglary.

While in prison, Malcolm was introduced to the Black Muslims, an offshoot of Islam that believes in separating whites and blacks. He changed his name to Malcolm X and was released in 1952. He became famous for his eloquent and often bitter speeches that denounced whites and white oppression.

Over time, Malcolm X came to embrace orthodox Islam, which calls for racial unity. He began to change his teachings, and split away from the Black Muslims. He was assassinated by Black Muslims in 1965.

Nelson Mandela
Statesman
1918-

Nelson Mandela is the founding father of South Africa's multiracial government. Before 1994, South Africa had a whites-only government that discriminated against the country's black majority. As a leader of the African National Congress (ANC), Mandela fought against the official government policy of *apartheid*, or racial separation. He spent 26 years in prison for his political activities. He was released in 1990.

Mandela shared the 1993 Nobel Peace Prize for his efforts to establish a fair, multiracial government in South Africa. In 1994, he was elected president of South Africa, a job that he held until 1999. Mandela's heroism and courage made him one of the most respected men in the world.

Mickey Mantle
Baseball Star
1931-1995

Mickey Mantle was a standout center fielder for the New York Yankees baseball team, as well as a home-run-hitting machine. He led the American League (AL) in home runs for four years, hitting 536 homers in his career. Mantle helped lead the Yankees to the World Series 12 times during his 18-year career, which began in 1951. He set a record for the most World Series home runs with 18.

Mantle had his best season in 1956, when he won the baseball's Triple Crown by leading the AL in batting average (.353), home runs (52), and runs batted in (130). He was elected to baseball's Hall of Fame in 1974.

Mao Zedong
Communist Dictator
1893-1976

In 1949, Mao Zedong (*MOW zuh-DONG*) became China's leader after his Communist Party seized power. The Communists had fought a long civil war against the Chinese Nationalists, and Mao's leadership in the war had often been brilliant. In 1934 and 1935, he led an army of 100,000 troops on a perilous 6,000-mile trek, known as the Long March, to the mountains of northern China.

Mao's policies later led to problems, such as food shortages that killed millions of Chinese. In the 1960s, Mao launched a campaign against intellectuals called the Cultural Revolution that led to years of bloody upheaval. He also set himself up as a godlike figure to be worshipped. Mao was one of the most influential figures of the 20th century.

Guglielmo Marconi
Inventor of Radio
1874-1937

In 1895, Guglielmo Marconi (*goo-LYEHL-moh mar-KOH-nee*) sent telegraph signals through the air—without wires—for the first time. The Italian inventor's new device was first used on ships. It allowed ships' crews to stay in touch with each other and with nearby ports. Marconi's new device saved many lives and is best remembered for alerting rescue ships during the 1912 *Titanic* disaster.

In 1909, Marconi shared the Nobel Prize for his work. By 1921, people could speak over radio waves. Commercial radio stations began broadcasting music, news, and entertainment. Almost overnight, the radio became a household appliance.

George C. Marshall
Soldier and Statesman
1880-1959

George C. Marshall is one of the greatest Americans of the 20th century. As the U.S. Army's chief of staff during World War II, he took a small, poorly funded force and, in a short time, turned it into the world's mightiest army. Key decisions by Marshall shaped the successful U.S. war effort.

In 1947, Marshall became secretary of state. At the time, the U.S. feared the spread of communism in Europe. Marshall proposed the European Recovery Program, which gave massive aid to countries suffering from the aftereffects of the war. That program, now known as the Marshall Plan, helped rebuild Europe. Marshall received the 1953 Nobel Peace Prize.

John Marshall
Supreme Court Chief Justice
1755-1835

John Marshall is the man most responsible for making the judicial branch a powerful part of the U.S. government. In 1800, President John Adams named Marshall the chief justice of the Supreme Court. At the time, the Supreme Court had little power or respect.

In 1803, Marshall wrote a decision in a case called *Marbury* v. *Madison*. That decision established the Supreme Court's power to strike down acts of Congress that conflict with the U.S. Constitution. This power, called judicial review, gave the Court the job of interpreting the Constitution. Not everyone accepted that idea in Marshall's time, but today it is recognized as a basic part of U.S. government and democracy.

Thurgood Marshall
First Black Supreme Court Justice
1908-1993

In 1967, Thurgood Marshall became the first African American to sit on the U.S. Supreme Court. Named to the bench by President Lyndon Johnson, Marshall voted consistently for liberal positions on such issues as capital punishment and affirmative action. He served for 24 years.

Before being named to the high court, Marshall had become famous as an attorney for the National Association for the Advancement of Colored People (NAACP). The NAACP used the courts to attack racial segregation—separate rules for blacks and whites. Marshall argued 32 segregation cases before the Supreme Court and won 29. One of them was *Brown* v. *Board of Education of Topeka*, which led to racially integrated public schools.

The Marx Brothers

Groucho (Julius)
1890-1977

Chico (Leonard)
1886-1961

Harpo (Arthur)
1888-1964

Zeppo (Herbert)
1901-1979

In the 1920s and 1930s, the Marx brothers were the most hilarious comedy team on stage or screen. Each brother played a character with a distinct personality: Groucho made clever remarks. Harpo, who never spoke, played the harp. Chico spoke with an exaggerated Italian accent and served as a mischievous interpreter for Harpo. Zeppo played the straight man, trying to stay above the craziness created by the others.

Together, the brothers produced mayhem that poked fun at rich and powerful people. The Marx brothers appeared in several Broadway shows and 13 movies, including *The Cocoanuts* (1929), *Monkey Business* (1931), and *Duck Soup* (1933).

Karl Marx
Philosopher
1818-1883

Karl Marx was the main author of *The Communist Manifesto* and *Das Kapital*. These famous books form the basis for communism and democratic socialism—movements that strongly influenced world politics in the 20th century.

Marx opposed capitalism, or private businesses, because it is often unfair. He predicted that poor workers would overthrow rich and middle-class people. Society would then become classless, he said, and government would become unnecessary.

Marx correctly identified capitalism's flaws. However, his solutions are unclear. They have often been used by communist dictators to oppress people, rather than free them as Marx intended. Marx died penniless and unaware of his future importance.

Charles H. Mayo
1865-1939

William J. Mayo
1861-1939

Charles H. Mayo and William J. Mayo, both doctors, were the sons of William W. Mayo, a successful and famous Minnesota surgeon. In the 1890s, the three Mayos pioneered the idea of bringing several medical specialists together, to give patients a more accurate diagnosis.

After William W. Mayo's death in 1911, his sons established the Mayo Clinic in Rochester, Minnesota. It is now one of the world's largest and most respected medical facilities—a complex of hospitals where hundreds of thousands of people are treated each year.

Willie Mays
Baseball Star
1931-

SAY HEY!

During the 1954 World Series, Cleveland Indians batter Vic Wertz slammed a ball into deep center field. Outfielder Willie Mays of the New York Giants (later the San Francisco Giants) turned and raced after it. Mays stunned everyone by making an incredible over-the-shoulder catch that fans still talk about today.

Mays's 22-year major-league career (1951-1973) was full of such electrifying moments, and his bat was as good as his glove. He racked up a career batting average of .302, and his 660 home runs put him third on the all-time career-homers list, behind Henry Aaron and Babe Ruth. Mays, a very likable man, was known to everyone as the "Say Hey Kid."

Joseph McCarthy
Controversial U.S. Senator
1908-1957

After World War II, the U.S. and the Soviet Union became enemies in a "cold war" of fear and mistrust. During the late 1940s, a few U.S. government officials were unmasked as spies who worked for the Soviet Union. Some Americans suspected that there were more spies, and Joseph McCarthy, a U.S. senator from Wisconsin, played on those fears. In 1950, he declared that hundreds of communists were working in the U.S. government. He had no evidence and never found any communists. However, he launched investigations that ruined reputations and created a nationwide climate of fear.

In 1954, McCarthy's excesses forced the Senate to strip him of his power. Today, the term *McCarthyism* is used to describe any effort to whip up suspicion or fear by making baseless accusations.

Cyrus McCormick
Reaping Machine Inventor
1809-1884

When Cyrus McCormick was growing up, farmers had to harvest their crops by using hand tools. It was a back-breaking process, and they could reap only two to three acres a day. McCormick's father tried to build a reaping machine, but finally gave up. McCormick took over his father's work. In 1831, he came up with a horse-drawn machine that could reap ten acres a day.

Cyrus McCormick's reaper allowed farmers to plant larger crops and make more money. McCormick continued to improve on his reaping machines, which revolutionized agriculture.

Mark McGwire
Home Run King
1963-

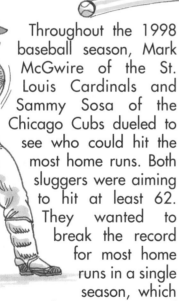

I CAN'T LOOK!

Throughout the 1998 baseball season, Mark McGwire of the St. Louis Cardinals and Sammy Sosa of the Chicago Cubs dueled to see who could hit the most home runs. Both sluggers were aiming to hit at least 62. They wanted to break the record for most home runs in a single season, which was 61—set in 1961 by Roger Maris of the New York Yankees.

The lead in the race changed hands several times, until September 8, 1998, when McGwire hit his 62nd home run. He eventually finished the season with 70 homers, the new single-season record. Sosa finished the season with 66.

Margaret Mead
Anthropologist
1901-1978

Margaret Mead became a famous anthropologist in the 1920s. *Anthropology* is the study of human cultures; Mead focused her attention on the peoples of the South Pacific. She lived among those peoples in order to understand their lifestyles and beliefs. Her writings showed how deeply a person's culture influences his or her behavior. Mead's most famous book is *Coming of Age in Samoa*.

Some of Mead's conclusions were controversial. Later researchers said that she interpreted information to suit her beliefs. However, Mead's work is still important, and she helped make anthropology more understandable to ordinary people.

George Meany
Union Leader
1894-1980

In the 1950s, organized labor in the U.S. was divided into two camps. The first was the American Federation of Labor (AFL), which was composed of skilled craft unions, such as plumbers and painters. The other was the Congress of Industrial Organizations (CIO), made up of mass-production workers, such as auto workers and coal miners.

In 1955, George Meany, head of the AFL, worked with leaders of the CIO to merge the two groups. The result was the AFL-CIO, which combined most labor unions into one organization. As leader of the AFL-CIO from 1955 to 1979, Meany rooted out corrupt unions as well as political radicals.

Medici Family
Rulers of Italy and France

Giovanni de' Medici
1360-1429

Lorenzo de' Medici
1449-1492

Cosimo de' Medici
1389-1464

Catherine de' Medici
1519-1589

The Medici (*MED-uh-chee*) family ruled Florence, Italy, from the 1400s to the early 1700s, when the city was at the height of its power. Three popes of the Roman Catholic church—Leo X, Clement VII, and Leo XI—came from the Medici family.

Giovanni de' Medici, a wealthy banker, established the dynasty. His son Cosimo seized control of Florence's politics. Lorenzo, often called "the Magnificent," was Cosimo's grandson. He made Florence a beautiful and powerful city. It became the driving force behind the Renaissance, or "rebirth," of Europe's arts and sciences after the Middle Ages. Catherine de' Medici (also known as Catherine des Médicis, the French version of her name) was Lorenzo's great-granddaughter. Married to King Henry II of France, she gave birth to three French kings and controlled French politics for 30 years before her death.

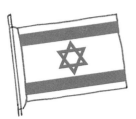

Golda Meir
Prime Minister of Israel
1898–1978

Golda Meir (*meh-EER*) helped to found the modern state of Israel. She was born in what is now Ukraine, and her family moved to the U.S. in 1906. Meir joined the Zionist movement, which sought to establish a Jewish state, called Israel, in Palestine. In 1921, she moved to Palestine and became a leader among the Zionists.

In 1948, part of Palestine became Israel. Meir served in several high offices until 1969, when she was elected prime minister. In 1973, during her time in office, a fourth war broke out between Israel and its Arab neighbors. Israel faced great danger, but Meir's diplomacy and firm leadership staved off disaster.

Herman Melville
Novelist
1819–1891

As a youth, Herman Melville traveled the world aboard whaling and U.S. Navy ships. He later used these adventures to fill the novels that made him famous, such as *Typee* and *White-Jacket*. In 1851, he published his most famous work, *Moby-Dick*. On one level, it was the story of the hunt for a white whale. On a deeper level, it reflects the struggle of humans against forces larger than themselves.

Moby-Dick was a flop when it was published, and Melville turned away from writing. The novel was rediscovered in the 1920s, and Melville has been considered a great author ever since.

Gregor Mendel
Groundbreaking Scientist
1822–1884

In 1843, Gregor Mendel was a Roman Catholic priest and high school science teacher in what is now the Czech Republic. He experimented with pea plants to see how they grew and inherited different traits.

He found that plants receive one gene from each parent that determined each trait. He also found that traits were either dominant (controlling) or recessive (having little or no effect). For instance, round seeds were dominant; wrinkled seeds were recessive. So a plant that inherited one gene for round seeds and one for wrinkled seeds would have round seeds.

Mendel's work was published in 1866 but ignored. In 1900, scientists rediscovered it and realized its importance.

Dmitri Mendeleev
Chemistry Pioneer
1834–1907

Michelangelo
Renaissance Genius
1475-1564

Dmitri Mendeleev *(DMEE-trih men-duh-LAY-uff)* was a Russian scientist who created the periodic table of elements that is used in chemistry. Elements are substances that cannot be broken down any further chemically, or that contain only one type of atom.

Hydrogen and oxygen are examples of elements. When put together, they make the compound called water. Everything around you is made from either an element or a compound of different elements.

Mendeleev's periodic table groups the elements together in several different ways, making them easier to understand. He left blank spaces to be filled in later, because he believed—accurately—that other elements would be discovered in the future.

Michelangelo designed the Florentine Pietá (above) for his own tomb. The hooded figure is a self-portrait.

Michelangelo *(MY-kuh-LAN-juh-loh)* di Lodovico Buonarroti Simoni was an accomplished painter, sculptor, architect, and poet. The intense, heroic figures he created made him the greatest artist of the Renaissance, which was the "rebirth" of Europe's art and sciences following the Middle Ages.

Born near Florence, Italy, Michelangelo's most famous painting was done in the Vatican's Sistine Chapel in Rome. On its ceiling and walls, he painted awe-inspiring frescoes (wall paintings) that interpret scenes from the Bible. His most famous sculpture, called the *David*, was also inspired by the Bible. It is widely considered the finest sculpture since the time of ancient Greece and Rome. Even many of Michelangelo's unfinished sculptures show tremendous power and beauty.

Edna St. Vincent Millay
Poet
1892-1950

Edna St. Vincent Millay was one of the most popular American poets of the 20th century. She was a master at writing sonnets, a poem that has 14 lines with a particular rhythm and rhyme scheme. In 1923, Millay won the Pulitzer Prize for her work.

Millay's early poems tended to focus on personal issues, such as love and religious experiences. Later in her life, her poems centered more on social issues, especially the tensions leading up to World War II (1939-1945). Millay also wrote plays, including an antiwar fantasy called *Aria da Capo*.

ARTHUR MILLER
PLAYWRIGHT
1915-

Arthur Miller is one of the greatest American playwrights of the 20th century. In 1949, he won the Pulitzer Prize for his best-known play, *Death of a Salesman* (pictured at right). It is a tragic story about a character named Willie Loman, a man who is destroyed by his pursuit of success. In 1953, Miller wrote *The Crucible*, a play about the Salem witch trials of the 1600s. At that time, the U.S. Congress was looking for communists in a way that seemed very much like the Salem witch hunts, when innocent people were accused of being witches.

Miller's other plays include *A View From the Bridge* and *Incident at Vichy*. Aside from his writing, Miller is also remembered for his marriage to film star Marilyn Monroe from 1956 to 1960.

A. A. Milne
Creator of Winnie the Pooh
1882-1956

In the 1920s, A. A. Milne wrote two of the most famous children's books ever, *Winnie-the-Pooh* and *The House at Pooh Corner*. Milne got the idea for his Winnie-the-Pooh stories from his son, Christopher Robin, and the boy's stuffed toys.

Alan Alexander Milne also wrote adult stories and plays, as well as two famous books of poetry for children, *When We Were Young* and *Now We Are Six*. However, it is the Pooh stories that made the English writer world-famous. Winnie-the-Pooh and his friends from the Hundred Acre Wood remain among the most popular characters ever created for children.

A. A. Milne with his son, Christopher Robin Milne

Minamoto Yoritomo
Ruler of Japan
1147-1199

Minamoto Yoritomo created the shogun system that ruled Japan for more than six centuries. He headed the Minamoto clan, which seized control of the country in 1185. Minamoto did not overthrow Japan's emperor. Instead, he forced the emperor to name him *shogun*, which is an abbreviation of a title meaning *barbarian-subduing general*.

The Minamotos lost power in 1219. However, other families continued to follow Minamoto Yoritomo's pattern. Technically, Japan's emperor was the most powerful person in Japan. However, the shogun, his family, and his advisers actually ran the country. The last shogun gave up that power in 1867.

Margaret Mitchell
Novelist
1900-1949

Margaret Mitchell wrote only one book, but that book was *Gone With the Wind*. Published in 1936, it quickly became one of the most popular American books of all time. The novel tells the story of two Southerners during the U.S. Civil War—the handsome and dashing Rhett Butler and the beautiful but temperamental Scarlett O'Hara.

Gone With the Wind won a Pulitzer Prize in 1937. The 1939 movie based on the book won 10 Academy Awards and for 20 years it earned more money than any other movie. However, both the book and movie have been criticized for their glorification of African American slavery and of such terrorist groups as the Ku Klux Klan.

James Monroe
Founding Father and 5th U.S. President
1758-1831

During the American Revolution (1775-1783), James Monroe distinguished himself with his bravery as an officer in the Continental Army. He also became a follower and lifelong friend of Thomas Jefferson, a fellow Virginian.

In 1817-1825, Monroe served as the country's fifth president. His two terms continued an "Era of Good Feeling," because there was little organized opposition to his political party, the Democratic-Republicans.

In 1823, Monroe warned European countries not to interfere with free countries in the Western Hemisphere. That policy, known as the Monroe doctrine, is the most famous of his presidency. It reduced European colonization in North and South America, and established U.S dominance on both Yontinents.

Marilyn Monroe
Movie Star
1926-1962

Marilyn Monroe's glamorous looks and her tragic death at age 36 have made her into a Hollywood legend. Born Norma Jean Mortenson, she changed her name at the start of her film career in 1948.

Monroe acted in 28 movies, including *All About Eve* and *Gentlemen Prefer Blondes*. Despite Monroe's intelligence, in the movies she was often cast as the dumb blonde. She was extremely unhappy in her personal life. Her marriages to baseball star Joe DiMaggio and playwright Arthur Miller ended in failure. In 1962, she died after taking an overdose of sleeping pills.

Joe Montana
Football Champion
1956-

Montezuma II
Aztec Emperor
1480-1520

Montezuma II ruled over the huge Aztec empire in what is now Mexico. In 1519, Spanish adventurers arrived, led by Hernán Cortés. At first Montezuma thought that Cortés might be a god and treated him kindly. However, Cortés soon made Montezuma a captive and began looting the Aztecs' rich treasuries.

The Aztecs believed that Montezuma had given in too easily, so they revolted. When Cortés brought out Montezuma to stop the rebellion, angry Aztecs hurled stones and injured him. Three days later, Montezuma was dead—perhaps from the stoning, perhaps from the harsh way he was treated by the Spanish. Within a few weeks, Montezuma's empire was completely under Spanish control.

Joe Montana was one of the greatest quarterbacks in National Football League (NFL) history. While in college, he led Notre Dame to the national championship in 1977. Drafted by the San Francisco 49ers in 1979, he helped make it the dominant team of the 1980s.

The 49ers went to the Super Bowl four times with Montana's passing and steady leadership. He was the first three-time winner of the Super Bowl's most valuable player (MVP) award, and he holds several Super Bowl passing records. Montana was voted into the Pro Bowl eight times during his 15-year career.

117

J. P. Morgan
Businessman
1837-1913

J. P. Morgan was probably the most powerful U.S. businessman in the late 1800s. He came from a wealthy family, and the core of his enormous wealth came from banking. Morgan was also fond of taking over struggling companies or industries and turning them around financially.

John Pierpont Morgan twice headed off national disaster during financial panics. In 1895, his company sold bonds to replenish the nearly bankrupt U.S. treasury. In 1907, he loaned money to banks to keep them from closing. Morgan's opulent home in New York City is now a library and museum.

TONI MORRISON
AUTHOR
1931-

Samuel F. B. Morse
Inventor of the Telegraph
1791-1872

Toni Morrison is one of today's most prominent African American novelists. She won a Pulitzer Prize in 1988 for her novel *Beloved*, a story about an escaped slave who is haunted by her past. In 1993, she won the Nobel Prize in literature, the first African American woman to do so. Morrison's novels reflect aspects of black life in the U.S. *Beloved*, for example, explores the complex feelings tied up in the issue of slavery. Her other books include *Tar Baby* and *Paradise*.

Morrison was born Chloe Anthony Wofford. She changed her first name to a shortened version of her middle name; Morrison comes from an early marriage.

Samuel Finley Breese Morse was an accomplished painter, doing portraits of President James Monroe and the Marquis de Lafayette. However, Morse had trouble earning a living as a painter, so he turned to inventing to make money.

Morse's most successful invention was the telegraph. On May 24, 1844, he sent a test message, "What hath God wrought!" from Washington to Baltimore. Within two decades, people thousands of miles apart were able to communicate instantly by telegraph. The telegraph's importance faded after telephones came into widespread use in the mid-20th century, and disappeared once fax machines became common in the late 20th century.

Grandma Moses
Folk Artist
1860-1961

During the 1930s, a famous art collector walking in Washington County, New York, saw a painting hanging in a drug-store window. He liked it so much, he asked who had painted it. He learned that it had been done by a 76-year-old self-taught artist named Anna Mary Robertson Moses. "Grandma Moses," as she was known, was soon displaying her paintings at New York City art galleries. Most are colorful portrayals of country life in the late 1800s. For many years, Moses had embroidered pictures on canvas with a needle and thread, but arthritis had forced her to stop. She turned to painting, which made her a world-famous celebrity.

Mother Goose
Storyteller
(dates unknown)

Nobody knows if Mother Goose really existed. If she did, several people could claim that title. One was Queen Bertha, the mother of Charlemagne, the ruler of medieval France. The queen, who died in A.D. 783, was known as "Goose-Footed Bertha" or "Queen Goose-foot."

In 1697, French author Charles Perrault published a collection of fairy stories—including "Little Red Riding Hood" and "Blue Beard"—that had the subtitle "Tales of My Mother Goose." Around that same time, a Boston woman named Mistress Elizabeth Goose (or Vergoose, or Vertigoose) reportedly became famous as a storyteller. In the 1760s, another Mother Goose book containing nursery rhymes was published in England. Countless others have been published since.

Wolfgang Amadeus Mozart
Composer
1756-1791

Wolfgang Amadeus Mozart *(MOTE-sahrt)* was one of the greatest musical geniuses ever. At age four, he could play a pianolike instrument called the harpsichord, and by age five he was composing music. As a child, he often performed before royal audiences, which were delighted to see the young prodigy.

Mozart mastered every instrument that he used, and composed more than 600 musical works—a remarkable output, especially considering the shortness of his life. Mozart died in poverty at age 36. Some of his most famous works include the operas *The Magic Flute* and *Don Giovanni*. His music remains among most beautiful and best-loved classical music ever written.

JOHN MUIR
NATURALIST AND EXPLORER
1838-1914

John Muir *(myur)* started the movement to conserve natural and wilderness areas in the U.S. Perhaps his biggest single contribution was to convince President Theodore Roosevelt, in 1903, to set aside 148 million acres of land for national forests. Before that, his lobbying of Congress resulted in the creation of Yosemite and Sequoia national parks.

Muir loved nature and spent much of his time exploring. He discovered a glacier in Alaska that has been named after him. Muir Woods, an ancient redwood forest near San Francisco, was also named in his honor. Muir founded the Sierra Club, which remains one of the most influential U.S. environmental groups.

Edward R. Murrow
Radio and Television Journalist
1908-1965

In 1940, World War II was raging and Nazi Germany was bombing London, England. Edward R. Murrow, a reporter for CBS Radio, made a series of famous broadcasts from London, telling Americans what was happening. Radio listeners could hear bombs exploding as Murrow eloquently described London's heroic defiance.

After the war, television took over radio's role. In 1954, Murrow's TV show *See It Now* covered an anticommunist crusade by U.S. Senator Joseph McCarthy. Murrow's broadcast helped to turn popular opinion against McCarthy. Many of the journalists who dominated TV news in its first three decades learned their trade from Murrow.

Benito Mussolini
Dictator
1883-1945

Benito Mussolini *(buh-NEE-toh MOO-suh-LEE-nee)*, a former journalist, helped drag Italy into World War II (1939-1945) on the side of Germany. Like Germany's leader, Adolf Hitler, Mussolini had dreams of creating a great empire. Unlike Hitler, however, Mussolini's armies were badly led and often defeated.

Mussolini was known as *Il Duce (il DOO-chay)*, or "the Leader," although his enemies called him the "Sawdust Caesar." His Fascist Party took power in 1922 and improved some areas of daily life, such as roads and railways. However, Mussolini also silenced newspapers and imprisoned political opponents. By the end of the war, Italy lay in ruins. Mussolini was captured by angry Italians and killed.

Napoleon I
Conqueror
1769-1821

Napoleon Bonaparte was one of the greatest military geniuses in history. However, his ambition to control a sprawling empire destroyed him.

In 1799, Napoleon became dictator of France in the wake of the French Revolution (1789-1799). His military conquests expanded France's borders, and his liberal reforms improved daily life in many ways. The *Code Napoléon*, for example, is still the basis for French law. In 1812, however, Napoleon invaded Russia and was badly defeated. In 1814, he was forced into exile. Napoleon tried to return to power, but was defeated by his enemies at the 1815 Battle of Waterloo. He was sent into exile again and died six years later.

Gamal Abdel Nasser
Statesman
1918-1970

Nefertiti
Queen of Ancient Egypt
Around 1350 B.C.

Nefertiti *(nef-ur-TEE-tee)* is one of the best-known queens of ancient Egypt. She was the chief wife of Akhenaton *(ahk-NAHT-n)*, the pharaoh. Together, they created sweeping religious reforms in Egypt.

In 1952, Gamal Abdel Nasser *(NAHS-ur)* led the military overthrow of Egypt's corrupt king. Within two years, Nasser ruled the country. He tried to unite the Arab world in a United Arab Republic, but his efforts proved unsuccessful. He also worked to improve daily life for ordinary people. Nasser took land from wealthy Egyptians and gave it to the poor. He also created the Aswan High Dam to control flooding on the Nile. A tireless champion of Arab causes, Nasser is still widely admired throughout the Middle East.

In 1967, Nasser started a war with Israel in which Egypt was badly beaten. He tried to resign after that, but was returned to office by popular demand.

Akhenaton threw out Egypt's wide variety of gods and goddesses and ordered that only Aton, the sun god, be worshipped. Many historians believe that Nefertiti was the priestess for Aton, a job normally reserved for the pharaoh.

Akhenaton and Nefertiti also oversaw radical changes in Egyptian art and culture. Many of these changes were reversed after Akhenaton died.

Jawaharlal Nehru
Founding Father of Modern India
1889-1964

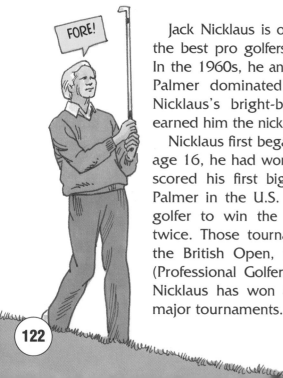

When India won its independence from Great Britain in 1947, Jawaharlal Nehru (*juh-WAH-hur-lahl NAY-roo*) became the country's first prime minister. It was a job that he held until his death. For the 20 years before 1947, Nehru and Mohandas K. Gandhi had led the resistance to British rule. The two men disagreed about many things, but both called for using nonviolent means to expel the British.

Nehru was known as *Pandit,* which means "the wise man" or "scholar." During the struggle for independence, he was imprisoned nine times. Nehru's family continued to dominate Indian politics long after his death.

Isaac Newton
Scientist
1642-1727

Isaac Newton was the greatest of all scientists before the 20th century. During an 18-month period from 1665 to 1667, this modest, absent-minded scientist made discoveries that revolutionized human thinking.

Newton did experiments that showed how color and light work. He helped create the branch of mathematics known as calculus. He invented the reflecting telescope. Most important of all, he showed that gravity was the force that held the universe together.

Many of Newton's ideas about gravity were later challenged by Albert Einstein, one of the few scientists who is considered Newton's equal. Yet Newton's work remains the bedrock upon which almost all modern science is based.

Jack Nicklaus
Golf Superstar
1940-

FORE!

Jack Nicklaus is one of the best pro golfers ever. In the 1960s, he and Arnold Palmer dominated the sport. Nicklaus's bright-blond hair and large body earned him the nickname "Golden Bear."

Nicklaus first began playing golf at age 10; by age 16, he had won a tournament. In 1962, he scored his first big win as a pro by beating Palmer in the U.S. Open. Nicklaus is the only golfer to win the top four golf tournaments twice. Those tournaments are the U.S. Open, the British Open, the Masters, and the PGA (Professional Golfers' Association) tournament. Nicklaus has won a record 20 titles in those major tournaments.

THAT GIVES ME AN IDEA!

Joseph Nicéphore Niépce
Inventor of Photography
1765-1833

HOLD STILL FOR EIGHT HOURS AND I WILL TAKE YOUR PHOTOGRAPH!

In the early 1800s, Joseph Nicéphore Niépce *(zhoh-ZEHF nee-say-FAWR nyehps)* , a French inventor, began looking for a way to produce permanent images of people and things. In 1826, he finally found a mix of light-sensitive chemicals that would make a faint image on a metal plate. The first surviving photograph ever taken shows the view outside Niépce's window.

Today, photographs are snapped in a fraction of a second. However, it took eight hours of exposure to sunlight for each of Niepce's photos to come out.

Niepce died before he could follow up on his work, but later inventors used it to create modern photography.

Florence Nightingale
Founder of Modern Nursing
1820-1910

As a young woman, Florence Nightingale became a nurse over the objections of her wealthy English family. In 1856, while Great Britain was fighting the Crimean War, Nightingale led a group of 39 nurses to tend to wounded British soldiers in Turkey.

Nightingale discovered that the military hospital in Turkey was filthy and infested with rats. Almost 50 percent of the wounded soldiers died from fever and illness. Nightingale cleaned up the hospital, improved health care, and reduced the death rate to two percent.

Nightingale, who soldiers called "the Lady with the Lamp," returned to Great Britain a hero. She became an international authority on nursing. She also founded the first nurses' training institution in the world.

Vaslav Nijinsky
Ballet Star
1889-1950

Vaslav Nijinsky *(VAHT-slaf nuh-ZHIN-skee)* was one of the greatest of all male ballet dancers. At age 17, he was considered the finest dancer in the world, with gravity-defying moves and tremendous body control. Nijinsky also choreographed, or designed, several dances that became the talk of Europe.

From 1907 to 1917, Nijinsky danced in ballets all over Europe and the U.S. He performed with the greatest ballerinas of his day. His career was cut short at age 29 by mental illness. From 1919 until his death, he lived in retirement in Europe.

Richard M. Nixon
Disgraced U.S. President
1913-1994

Richard M. Nixon is the only U.S. president ever to resign from office. While Nixon, a Republican, was running for re-election in 1972, members of his campaign committee broke into the Democratic Party's headquarters at Washington's Watergate Hotel. They were caught. Nixon broke the law by helping to cover up the White House's involvement in the break-in.

After nearly two years of investigations and court cases, the so-called Watergate scandal forced Nixon resign in August 1974. Along the way, the public learned that Nixon had used other illegal and underhanded methods to fight his political opponents. Nixon is widely seen as a tragic figure—a dedicated, intelligent man who caused his own downfall.

I AM *NOT* A CROOK!

Kwame Nkrumah
African Revolutionary Leader
1909-1972

Kwame Nkrumah *(KWAHM-ee en-KROO-muh)* helped lead the resistance to British colonial rule in West Africa during the late 1940s. He organized a series of strikes that crippled the economy of Britain's colonies. By 1957, the resistance that Nkrumah led forced the British to leave.

Nkrumah became the first president of the newly independent country of Ghana (formerly the Gold Coast) in 1960. At first, he tried to improve life for ordinary people, and fought for the creation of a United States of Africa. However, he soon became an oppressive, corrupt dictator. Nkrumah was overthrown by Ghana's army in 1966.

Alfred Nobel
Creator of the Nobel Prizes
1833-1896

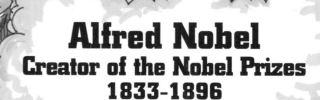

Alfred Nobel *(noh-BELL)* was a Swedish chemist who invented dynamite. In the 1860s, chemists were looking for a way to make liquid nitroglycerin easier to use. Nitroglycerin was likely to blow up if it was shaken or mishandled. Nobel mixed it with a powder that made it stable. He called the result dynamite and sold it to businesses, miners, and armies.

Nobel became fabulously wealthy. Toward the end of his life, he funded an annual prize for people who helped humanity through good works, literature, or scientific research. The first Nobel prizes were awarded in 1901. They remain the most prestigious prizes in the world.

Nostradamus
Astrologer and Doctor
1503~1566

I PREDICT THAT YOU WILL ENJOY THIS BOOK!

Many people believe that Nostradamus (NOHS-truh-DAHM-us) could see into the future. Nostradamus was the Latin pen name of Michel de Nostredame, a French physician. His reputation for prophesy is tied to a book that he wrote called *Centuries*.

Published in 1555, *Centuries* supposedly describes events from the mid-1500s until the end of the world. Some modern writers say that Nostradamus predicted events such as Adolf Hitler's rise to power and the assassination of U.S. President John F. Kennedy. However, critics say that *Centuries* is so unclear that it can be read several different ways. Also, some predictions that seemed accurate were really mistranslations of what Nostradmus wrote.

Rudolf Nureyev
Ballet Star
1938-1993

Rudolf Nureyev (*nuh-RAY-yuff*) was one of the most important male ballet dancers of the late 1900s. He began dancing at age 11 in his native country, the Soviet Union. However, Nureyev hated the lack of freedom under the Soviet Union's communist system. In 1961, when his ballet company was touring in France, he slipped past his security guards and escaped to freedom.

After that, Nureyev toured throughout Europe and the U.S. He danced more than 100 roles, and he formed a special partnership with British ballet star Margot Fonteyn. Nureyev also created new dances for such traditional ballets as *The Nutcracker* and *Don Quixote*.

ANNIE OAKLEY
SHARPSHOOTER
1860-1926

Nobody could shoot a gun as well as Annie Oakley. For more than 16 years, she was one of the star attractions in Buffalo Bill's Wild West show. Oakley could hit a dime tossed in the air or fill a playing card with holes before it hit the ground. She once shot a cigarette out of the mouth of Germany's crown prince.

Born Phoebe Ann Moses in Ohio, she started shooting at age eight to kill game and make money. She took the stage name Annie Oakley, and joined Buffalo Bill's show in 1885. Oakley, who stood only five feet tall, was known as "Little Sure Shot."

Sandra Day O'Connor
First Female Supreme Court Justice
1930-

In 1981, President Ronald Reagan named Arizona judge Sandra Day O'Connor to the U.S. Supreme Court, making her the first woman to hold that job. She had previously served as a state senator, and was the first woman to be majority leader of Arizona's state senate.

O'Connor received her law degree from Stanford University in 1952. Despite graduating with high grades, at first she was passed over for many jobs because of her gender. Her early Supreme Court opinions were strongly conservative. However, they have since become more moderate.

Georgia O'Keeffe
Experimental Artist
1887-1986

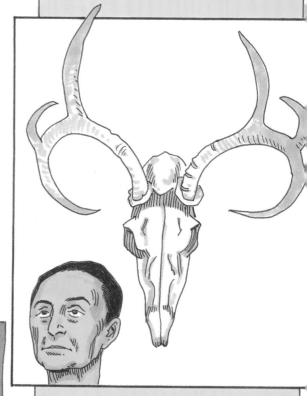

Georgia O'Keeffe's still-life paintings are well-known for their clear colors and nature themes. O'Keeffe loved the American Southwest, and frequently used desert flowers or old cow bones as her subjects. O'Keeffe also created many abstract paintings, (paintings in which there was no identifiable subject).

During the 1910s, O'Keeffe was an art teacher in Texas. Photographer Alfred Stieglitz became interested in her work, and he displayed them in his New York gallery. O'Keeffe and Stieglitz later married. In 1949, O'Keeffe moved to New Mexico. Eleven years after her death, the Georgia O'Keeffe Museum was established in Santa Fe, New Mexico.

Eugene O'Neill
Playwright
1888–1953

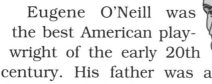

Eugene O'Neill was the best American playwright of the early 20th century. His father was a successful actor, and the family traveled widely with him. As a young man, O'Neill drifted through a series of low-paying jobs, and his lifestyle almost destroyed his health. While recovering, he decided to become a playwright. His first play, *Bound East for Cardiff*, opened in New York in 1916.

All but one of O'Neill's 35 plays are dramas. They include *The Iceman Cometh* and *Long Day's Journey Into Night*. Four of his plays won Pulitzer Prizes. In 1936, O'Neill was awarded the Nobel Prize for literature.

Jacqueline Bouvier Kennedy Onassis
U.S. First Lady
1929-1994

Jacqueline Bouvier Kennedy Onassis, known as Jackie, rose to fame as the wife of President John F. Kennedy. As a young, beautiful First Lady, Jackie set fashion trends in the early 1960s. Her grace and charm aided her husband's relationship with world leaders. However, tragedy struck in 1963, when President Kennedy was shot to death while riding next to her in an open car.

The country's sorrow and sympathy for Jackie Kennedy turned to surprise in 1968, when she married Aristotle Onassis, a Greek shipping millionaire. Their stormy marriage ended in 1975, when he died. Although Jackie Onassis became a highly respected book editor, she remained the target of gossip magazines all her life.

J. Robert Oppenheimer
Father of the Atomic Bomb
1904-1967

PAPA!

During World War II (1939-1945), the U.S. feared that Nazi Germany or Japan might build an atomic bomb. So U.S. government officials asked J. Robert Oppenheimer, a brilliant scientist, to help them beat the enemy to the punch. As leader of the top-secret Manhattan Project, Oppenheimer gathered most of the world's leading scientists to work on the problem.

In August 1945, the result of their labors was used in combat. Atomic bombs were exploded over two cities in Japan. The bombs had a horrifying effect, killing more than 340,000 people. However, they also helped bring World War II to an abrupt end.

GEORGE ORWELL
AUTHOR
1903-1950

George Orwell was the pen name of Eric Blair, an English novelist and critic. He wrote two of the most important novels of the 20th century—*1984* and *Animal Farm*. In *1984*, Orwell shows a nightmare world of the future where the government has taken away all privacy and allows no criticism. *Animal Farm* is a fable about living without freedom under communism. Both novels show how dictators turn the truth on its head and crush individual feelings and ideas to preserve their power.

Besides the novels, Orwell was well-known for his essays and books criticizing the unfairness that he saw in British society.

"BIG BROTHER IS WATCHING YOU."
(from *1984*)

"ALL ANIMALS ARE CREATED EQUAL—I'M MORE EQUAL THAN THE OTHERS!"
(from *Animal Farm*)

I WROTE THOSE LINES!

Elisha Graves Otis
Inventor of the Safe Elevator
1811-1861

Elisha Graves Otis did not invent the elevator—he invented the brake that stops an elevator if its cable should break. Otis gave a dramatic demonstration of his device at the 1854 Crystal Palace Exposition in New York City. He rode up in an elevator that had one side visible to the audience. After hoisting the elevator halfway up, he had someone cut the cable! The breathless audience watched Otis's device save him from a horrible death.

Otis's brake let architects use elevators in the new skyscrapers, which became fashionable in the 1870s. Without it, such tall buildings would not have been possible.

Jesse Owens
Olympic Hero
1913-1980

The 1936 Berlin Olympics were supposed to be a showcase for Adolf Hitler's belief that "Aryan" whites were superior to other races. That belief was shattered by Jesse Owens, an African American track-and-field sensation. Owens won four gold medals and set a world record in the long jump. Hitler left the Olympic stadium rather than congratulate a black person.

Owens returned to the U.S. a hero, but at that time black athletes had few ways of making money. Owens worked in public relations and community service. In 1976, he was awarded the Presidential Medal of Freedom.

Satchel Paige
Negro League Pitching Great
1906-1982

Before 1947, professional baseball was divided by race. Satchel Paige and other black athletes could play only in the Negro leagues. Paige was one of the greatest pitchers. His scorching fastball led the Kansas City Monarchs to four straight championships in the 1930s.

Leroy Robert Paige got his nickname by working as a baggage handler at a train station. (A *satchel* is a type of suitcase or shoulder bag.) In 1948, at age 40—old for a ball player—Paige signed with the Cleveland Indians, a previously whites-only team. He helped lead them to the World Series. He was elected to the National Baseball Hall of Fame in 1971.

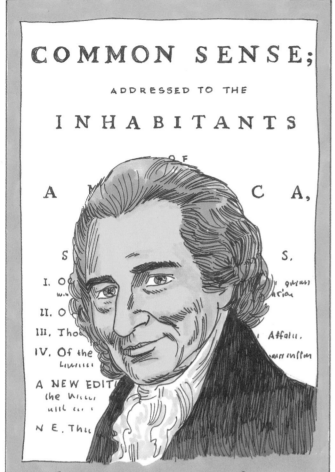

Thomas Paine
Founding Father
1737-1809

In the 1770s, Thomas Paine wrote *Common Sense* and *The Crisis*, two pamphlets that electrified colonial America. In them, Paine made brilliant arguments for the colonies to win independence from Great Britain, greatly boosting support for the American Revolution (1775-1783). *The Crisis* begins with the famous words, "These are the times that try men's souls."

Paine later went to France, where he became a leading figure in the French Revolution (1789-1799). He was an unselfish man who strongly believed in freedom and democracy, but he also made many enemies. Paine believed in God, but criticized Christianity and other religions. Such opinions made him unpopular, and he died an outcast in the United States.

Arnold Palmer
Golf Superstar
1929-

Arnold Palmer is widely credited with making professional golf a popular sport. He was the first golfer to win the Masters championship four times. In 1967, he became the first professional golfer to win more than $1 million in prize money.

Palmer was loved by the public. On golf courses, he was followed by a group of fans who came to be known as "Arnie's Army."

Palmer, who began golfing when he was three years old, attended Wake Forest University on a golf scholarship.

Palmer was a dominant player throughout the 1960s. His main rival on the golf course was Jack Nicklaus.

CHARLIE PARKER
JAZZ GENIUS
1920–1955

During his short, troubled life, Charlie "Bird" Parker became one of the greatest jazz musicians of all. He helped invent a type of music called be-bop, a fast-paced, improvisational style that has influenced and inspired saxophone players and other musicians for generations.

Parker grew up in Kansas City, Missouri, where he taught himself to play the alto saxophone. By the 1940s, he was one of the hottest jazz musicians in the world, playing with other greats, such as Dizzy Gillespie and Thelonious Monk.

Parker became addicted to heroin, a dangerous drug. His addiction caused problems in his career and personal life, and destroyed his health. Eventually, it took his life at the young age of 35.

Rosa Parks
Civil-rights Pioneer
1913–

On December 1, 1955, Rosa Parks did something earthshaking—she refused to give up her seat on a city bus to a white passenger. At the time, blacks living in Montgomery, Alabama, were required to give up their seats to whites.

Parks, a seamstress and civil-rights activist, was arrested. Other African Americans rallied to her cause: For a year, they refused to ride Montgomery's buses. Martin Luther King Jr. became their leader. In 1956, courts ruled that Montgomery had to end its prejudiced ways. Parks's action led to similar protests across the nation. She is often called the mother of the civil-rights movement.

Blaise Pascal
Philosopher and Scientist
1623-1662

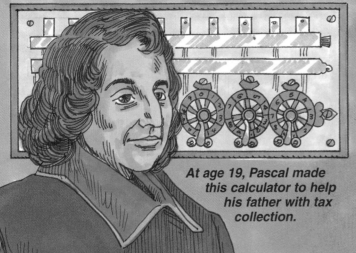

At age 19, Pascal made this calculator to help his father with tax collection.

As a young boy in France, Blaise Pascal *(blaze pas-KAL)* was recognized as a genius. At age 12, he mastered difficult geometry problems and, at 17, he wrote an important work on the subject. As an adult scientist, Pascal helped explain how water pressure works. He also helped prove that air has weight, and that a vacuum can be created. (A *vacuum* is a space where nothing—not even air—exists.)

Pascal was also a philosopher and a passionate believer in Christianity. His works defended the Christian faith. They also greatly influenced the way the French language was written.

Louis Pasteur
Scientist
1822–1895

Few scientists have helped as many people as Louis Pasteur (*pas-TUR*). He proved that germs cause disease and he showed where they come from—two of his greatest accomplishments. Pasteur also created a process to keep milk and other drinks from turning sour quickly by using controlled heat. This process is called pasteurization.

Pasteur saved France's important silk industry by curing a disease that was killing off silkworms. He also discovered a vaccine for rabies. In 1888, so many people were grateful to Pasteur that they created the Pasteur Institute in Paris. Today, it is dedicated to fighting diseases.

George Patton
U.S. Army General
1885-1945

George Patton was one of the most colorful and talented generals of World War II. He is best remembered for his leadership of the U.S. Third Army in France. When he took command, the U.S. and its allies were bogged down, unable to move. Patton engineered a breakout that sent the German army reeling. Patton's fierceness earned him the nickname "Blood and Guts."

Bad judgment got Patton into trouble. He once outraged the public when he slapped a battle-weary soldier and called him a coward. He also criticized U.S. policy in public. Patton was badly injured in a car accident and died just months after the war's end.

Luciano Pavarotti
Opera Star
1935-

Luciano Pavarotti (*loo-chee-AHN-oh pah-vuh-RAHT-tee*) gave up a career as a schoolteacher to become one of the most popular opera stars of the 20th century. He appeared in his first big role in 1961; by 1965, he was well known as an international star.

Pavarotti has a rich tenor voice, and he can make singing difficult high notes look easy. In 1990, he began teaming up with fellow singers Plácido Domingo (*doh-MEEN-goh*) and José Carreras (*cuh-REHR-rahs*) to form an informal group called the Three Tenors. Their concerts always sell out and their albums have become the best-selling classical recordings of all time.

Ivan Pavlov
Scientist
1849-1936

Ivan Pavlov (*PAHV-loff*) is best remembered as the Russian scientist who could make dogs drool. Pavlov taught his dogs to expect food whenever they heard  a bell ring. The idea of food made the dogs drool in expectation. Pavlov's research was important because it showed that reflexes could be trained to behave a certain way.

In 1904, Pavlov won the Nobel Prize for medicine. In 1917, communists took over Russia. Pavlov was a constant critic of the communists, who usually killed or imprisoned their opponents. However, Pavlov was such an important scientist that communist leaders allowed him to continue working until his death.

Polar Explorers

Robert Peary
1856-1920

Matthew Henson
1867-1955

On April 6, 1909, American explorer Robert Peary (*PIHR-ee*), his assistant Matthew Henson, and four Inuits (Eskimos) reached the North Pole. It was the first time anyone had ever done so. Henson planted the U.S. flag there, and Peary soon telegraphed back the message, "Stars and Stripes nailed to the North Pole." Upon returning home, however, Peary found that another explorer, Dr. Frederick Cook, claimed to have beaten him by five days. Scientists studied the records of both sides. When they concluded that Peary was the true winner, he was widely celebrated as a hero.

In the 1980s, some scientists claimed that Peary's navigation had been off by as much as 60 miles. Once again, experts studied the matter and agreed that Peary's team really did reach the North Pole.

Henson was a key member of the team, and may even have reached the Pole first, but neither he nor the Inuits received credit in the years that followed. Peary was kind to Henson in private, but refused to give anyone else public credit for the expedition's success. Much of the problem was race: Henson was black, and few white people in the early 1900s could accept a black hero. Nevertheless, toward the end of his life, Henson finally did receive credit for his daring accomplishments.

Pelé
Soccer Superstar
1940-

Pelé *(peh-LAY)* is the greatest soccer player in history. He led his native country of Brazil to World Cup soccer titles in 1958, 1962, and 1970. He is the only man to play on three world championship teams.

Born Edson Arantes do Nascimento *(ED-sone ah-RAHN-ches doh nah-sih-MEN-toh)*, Pelé was a master at scoring and passing. He played for most of his career in Brazil, but joined the New York Cosmos of the North American Soccer League (NASL) in 1975. In 1977, Pelé led the Cosmos to a league championship, then retired. During Pelé's professional career, he scored an amazing 1,281 goals in 1,363 games.

William Penn
Founder of Pennsylvania
1644-1718

William Penn created the English colony that later became the state of Pennsylvania. He was a wealthy man and an outspoken member of the Quakers—a small group of Christians who were being harshly attacked in England at that time. With the king's permission, Penn set up his new colony as a place where all religious beliefs would be tolerated.

The democratic government that Penn created in Pennsylvania influenced later colonies. His dealings with the local Native Americans was so fair that they never attacked Pennsylvania colonists.

Penn's great achievements have been immortalized in the name *Pennsylvania*, which means "Penn's Woods."

Pericles
Leader of Ancient Athens
490-429 B.C.

Pericles *(PEHR-uh-kleez)* was the greatest democratic leader of ancient times. His wisdom, eloquence, and honesty led Athens to its golden age, which is also called the Age of Pericles.

Pericles opened the democratic government of Athens to poor, average people, allowing them to hold public office and serve on juries. He also made Athens strong militarily and built famous temples, including the Parthenon, which still stands.

The power of Athens threatened nearby Sparta; in 431 B.C., the two Greek city-states went to war. Pericles died of disease in 429 B.C. Athens eventually lost the war in 404 B.C. The city recovered somewhat, but never recaptured its former Periclean glory.

Frances Perkins
First Female Cabinet Member
1882-1965

Frances Perkins was already a champion of the poor when she witnessed a fire at the Triangle Shirtwaist Company on March 25, 1911, in New York City. Unsafe conditions at that factory led to the deaths of 146 girls and women working there. The horror of that disaster inspired Perkins to work hard for labor reforms.

During the 1920s, Perkins helped win better labor laws for New York, and she served in high-ranking state jobs. In 1933, President Franklin Roosevelt named her U.S. labor secretary. That made her the first woman to serve in a president's cabinet (the group of advisers and people in charge of federal departments).

Peter the Great
Creator of Modern Russia
1672-1725

When Peter the Great became czar *(zahr)*, or ruler, of Russia in 1682, his country was the most backward in Europe. Few of its people were educated and it had little contact with other countries. Peter reformed Russia's government, established the city of St. Petersburg, and created schools, museums, and libraries. He also modernized the army and used it to expand Russia's borders.

A great admirer of European culture, Peter the Great introduced many European customs to Russia. His critics said that he did little to help ordinary Russians, who suffered from poverty and high taxes. Most historians agree, however, that Peter transformed Russia into a major European power.

John Pershing
Led U.S. Forces in World War I
1860-1948

In 1886, John J. Pershing graduated from the U.S. Military Academy at West Point and soon began fighting Apache Indians. He rose quickly through the army's ranks. He earned his nickname, "Black Jack," because he commanded an all-black regiment for a while.

In 1917, the U.S. entered World War I (1914-1918). Pershing was asked to lead the American Expeditionary Force (AEF) in Europe. He built the tiny U.S. Army into a fighting force of more than two million men, and those troops helped turn the tide against Germany. After the war, Pershing was named General of the Armies, the highest rank that a U.S. Army officer can attain.

PABLO PICASSO
ARTIST
1881–1973

Pablo Picasso (pih-KAHS-oh) is perhaps the most famous artist of the 20th century. Influenced by African art, he helped pioneer the painting style known as cubism in 1907. Cubism's goal was to show one subject from different angles at the same time. For instance, a cubist painter might show a woman's face as a series of geometric shapes and jagged edges.

Picasso's paintings, sculptures, drawings, engravings, and ceramics influenced other artists of his time—and still influence artists today. Perhaps his greatest masterpiece is a mural called *Guernica*. Picasso, who was born in Spain, painted it in 1937 to protest the bombing of the Spanish city of Guernica during the Spanish Civil War (1936–1939).

Plato
Philosopher of Ancient Greece
427-347 B.C.

Along with Socrates and Aristotle, Plato (PLATE-oh) is one of the most famous philosophers of the ancient world. He was an Athenian nobleman.

Plato began his career in philosophy as a pupil of the Socrates. In fact, without Plato's writings, we would know very little about Socrates. Plato founded a school called the Academy in Athens, and served as Aristotle's teacher for many years.

Over many centuries, Plato's ideas have shaped philosophical discussions on many topics, ranging from politics to the existence of the soul. His teachings also had a huge influence on Christianity, Judaism, and Islam. Religious thinkers have used Plato's ideas to help explain hard-to-understand questions of faith.

Plutarch
Historian and Writer
A.D. 46-120

Today, our knowledge of ancient Greece and Rome is sketchy and incomplete. However, we would know even less if it had not been for the writings of a historian named Plutarch (PLOO-tark).

Plutarch was a Greek scholar who lived during the time when Rome ruled over Greece. He wrote several biographies on famous Greeks and Romans that are invaluable to scholars today. Plutarch was a lively writer who could bring his subjects to life. Modern historians have discovered that some details in Plutarch's writings were wrong. However, he remains one of the most important of all ancient writers.

Pocahontas
Native American Hero
1595–1617

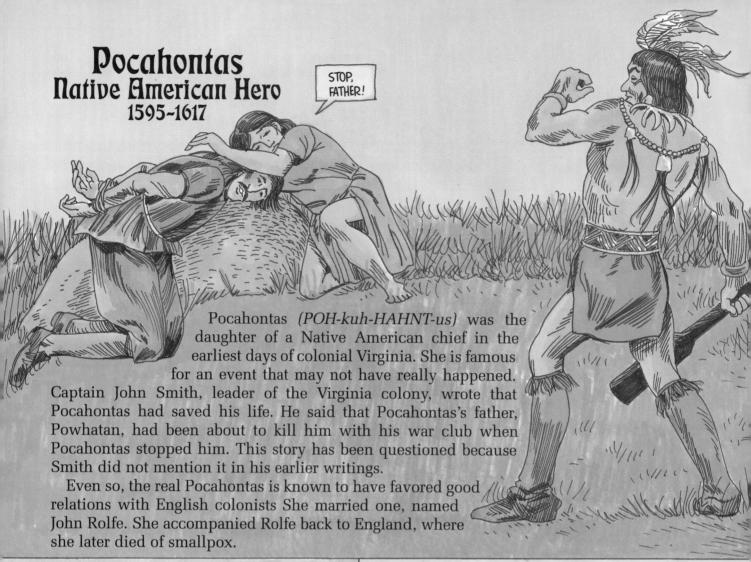

Pocahontas (*POH-kuh-HAHNT-us*) was the daughter of a Native American chief in the earliest days of colonial Virginia. She is famous for an event that may not have really happened. Captain John Smith, leader of the Virginia colony, wrote that Pocahontas had saved his life. He said that Pocahontas's father, Powhatan, had been about to kill him with his war club when Pocahontas stopped him. This story has been questioned because Smith did not mention it in his earlier writings.

Even so, the real Pocahontas is known to have favored good relations with English colonists She married one, named John Rolfe. She accompanied Rolfe back to England, where she later died of smallpox.

Edgar Allan Poe
Master of Horror Stories
1809-1849

Edgar Allan Poe is forever connected with stories of the strange and ghostly. He wrote some of the best-known horror stories of all time, including "The Fall of the House of Usher" and "The Tell-Tale Heart." Poe's brilliant writing made him one of the first American writers to win an international reputation.

Poe is also well-remembered for his poems, especially "The Raven" and "Annabel Lee." Poe is considered the inventor of the detective story, with his short story "The Murders in the Rue Morgue." During Poe's brief life, he enraged many other writers with his criticisms of them.

JACKSON POLLOCK
ARTIST
1912-1956

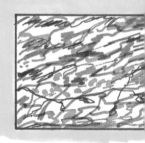

Jackson Pollock has become one of America's best-known abstract painters. Abstract artists do not try to represent reality. Instead, they express their ideas using unusual shapes and colors. Pollock was known as "Jack the Dripper" because he liked to use bold paint splashes and splatters. He usually put his giant canvases on the floor, allowing him to throw and splash paint with more dramatic effects.

Pollock had a huge impact on other artists. He made little money from sales of his paintings while he was alive. Today, however, his paintings sell for millions of dollars each.

Sidney Poitier
Film Star
1927-

In the 1950s, Sidney Poitier (*PWAH-tee-ay*) became the first black actor to win fame as a leading man. He grew up in the Bahamas. At first, his heavy accent made it hard for him to win acting roles in the U.S., but Poitier learned to speak American English by imitating voices that he heard on the radio. He soon became the top black actor in the country.

Poitier's work in 1958 film *The Defiant Ones* made him the first African American nominated for an Academy Award for Best Actor. In 1963, he won the Best Actor award for *Lilies of the Field*. A 1967 film, *The Man Who Came to Dinner*, broke new ground with its examination of racial issues.

Marco Polo
Adventurer and Explorer
1254-1324

Marco Polo was born into a family of merchants in Venice, Italy. At age 17, he set out for China with his father and uncle, to look for trading opportunities in that distant land. It was the start of a 24-year adventure in which Polo traveled more than 15,000 miles.

At that time, few people ever left their hometowns, and they knew very little about faraway places. When Polo returned home, he wrote about his travels in China and Asia. Europeans were astounded by his tales of China's great wealth, learning, and technological know-how. Polo's book inspired many later explorers, including Christopher Columbus.

Beatrix Potter
Children's Author
1866-1943

HI, MS. POTTER!

In 1900, Helen Beatrix Potter wanted to help a sick child. So, with her own money, she published *The Tale of Peter Rabbit*—a story that she had written years before. The book included illustrations that she had painted—gentle water-color pictures of Peter and his friends.

Within a few years, Beatrix Potter had become one of the world's leading children's authors. Her characters—which include Jemima Puddle-Duck, Mrs. Tiggy-Winkle, and Benjamin Bunny—remain popular with children. Potter, who loved animals, got the inspiration for her 25 books partly from her own collection of pets.

Elvis Presley
The King of Rock 'n' Roll
1935-1977

In 1953, Elvis Presley went to a Memphis, Tennessee, studio to record a song as a present for his mother. His voice was so good that the studio owner asked him to sing professionally. By 1956, Presley had become America's rock 'n' roll sensation. "Love Me Tender," "Hound Dog," and other Presley songs rocketed to the top of the charts. His notorious hip-shaking moves during concerts thrilled teenagers and offended many adults.

Forty-five of Presley's records sold more than one million copies each, and he made 33 movies. Presley, who became addicted to prescription drugs and ate large portions of greasy foods, died of heart failure when he was just 42.

Joseph Pulitzer
Publisher
1847-1911

In the late 1800s, Joseph Pulitzer (PUHL-ut-sir) was one of the most powerful publishers in the U.S. His *St. Louis Post-Dispatch* newspaper became famous for its attacks on political corruption and sensational reporting, and it made Pulitzer a rich man.

Pulitzer, who also owned the *New York World*, carried on a feud with William Randolph Hearst, who owned the *New York Morning Journal*. Both newspapers used questionable and often sleazy stories to attract readers. Those methods became known as "yellow journalism."

In Pulitzer's will, he left money to create the Pulitzer Prizes, which have been awarded each year since 1917. They are now the most sought-after awards in U.S. journalism, literature, drama, and music.

Pu Yi
China's Last Emperor
1906-1967

Pu Yi *(poo yee)* led a strange and tragic life. At age two, he was made emperor of China. However, wars and political upheaval had weakened China so much that revolution broke out. In 1912, at age six, Pu Yi (also known as Henry Pu-yi) gave up his throne, ending a *dynasty* (family line of rulers) that dated back to 1644.

When Japan invaded China in the 1930s, Pu Yi agreed to become a puppet emperor over part of the conquered territory. After Japan's defeat in 1945, Pu Yi was imprisoned until 1959. He spent the last eight years of his life as a gardener in Beijing, China's capital. Pu Yi's life was the focus of *The Last Emperor* (1987), an award-winning movie.

Ernie Pyle
War Journalist
1900-1945

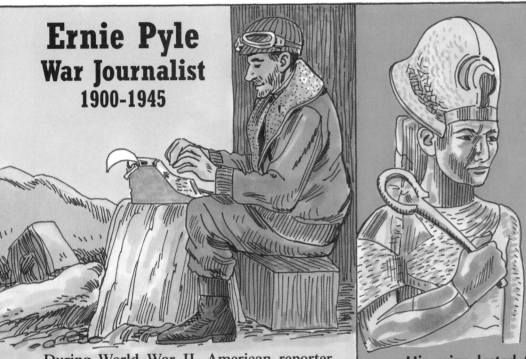

Ramses II
Pharaoh of Ancient Egypt
1200s B.C.

During World War II, American reporter Ernie Pyle wrote about the lives of ordinary U.S. GIs in combat. He lived with soldiers, sailors, and airmen, and told Americans back home what he learned. Hundreds of newspapers across the U.S. carried his articles. In 1944, he won a Pulitzer Prize for his work.

Pyle's columns were put together and published in books—including *Here Is Your War* and *Brave Men*—that became best sellers. Pyle died during the battle of Okinawa, just four months before the war ended. However, his personal style of reporting remained a strong influence on later war journalists.

Ramses II *(RAM-seez)* was one of the greatest leaders of ancient Egypt. His reign lasted from about 1279 B.C. to 1212 B.C. At first, Ramses focused on a long, bloody struggle with the Hittites, a powerful kingdom in the Middle East. Ramses won control of some land from the Hittites, but the war ended in a draw.

The last part of Ramses' rule was devoted to building huge monuments. Tourists today can still visit the Great Hall of the Temple of Amon-Re and the rock temples at Abu Simbel. Ramses is believed to be the pharaoh in the Bible who gave the Israelites their freedom, but historians are unsure.

A. Philip Randolph
Union and Civil-rights Leader
1889-1979

A. Philip Randolph believed that unions could help African Americans win equal rights. His efforts gave blacks greater economic power in the U.S. In the 1920s, railway porters—men who carried bags for passengers—were mostly black. Randolph organized them into a powerful union, the Brotherhood of Sleeping Car Porters. The union won higher salaries and better working conditions for porters.

As World War II approached, U.S. industries geared up for the war effort. Wartime factory jobs, however, went only to white workers. Randolph warned President Franklin Roosevelt that thousands of blacks would march on Washington if the situation did not change. In June 1941, Roosevelt ordered that defense and government jobs be opened to blacks.

Randolph continued to work for equal rights until illness forced him to retire in 1968.

Jeannette Rankin
First Female to Serve in Congress
1880-1973

Montana

In 1916, Jeannette Rankin became the first woman elected to the U.S. Congress. A Republican from Montana, she was deeply committed to women's rights and to opposing all war.

In 1917, Rankin was one of only 49 members of Congress to vote against the U.S. entering World War I (1914-1918). That unpopular stand cost Rankin her seat in the House of Representatives.

On December 7, 1941, Japan launched a sneak attack against the U.S. Rankin, who had been reelected to the House just a year before, was the only member of Congress to vote against declaring war on Japan.

Ronald Reagan
40th U.S. President
1911-

Ronald Reagan first became famous as a Hollywood actor, appearing in more than 50 films. Perhaps the most memorable was *Knute Rockne-All American*, in which Reagan played a character called George "the Gipper" Gipp.

In the 1960s, Reagan entered Republican politics and became governor of California. His conservative policies made him controversial, but his sunny disposition greatly boosted his popularity. He was elected president in 1980, and served two terms. He took a strong stand against the Soviet Union, and has been credited with helping cause its 1991 collapse. His speaking skills earned him the nickname "the Great Communicator."

Rembrandt
Artist
1606–1669

Rembrandt was one of the greatest artists of all time. He was a master of using light and shadows to create unforgettable images.

Rembrandt's full name was Rembrandt van Rijn *(REMbrant vahn ryne)*. With equal grace, he could paint scenes showing everyday life or portraits of rich and famous people. The sheer number of works that he produced is amazing: At least 600 paintings, 300 etchings, and 1,400 drawings are said to be Rembrandt creations.

Rembrandt's brilliance was recognized during his lifetime, and he became famous. His best-known works include *The Night Watch*, *Blinding of Samson*, and *The Return of the Prodigal Son*.

Walter Reuther
Labor Leader
1907–1970

Walter Reuther *(ROO-thur)* was a visionary U.S. labor leader. He helped make the United Auto Workers of America (UAW) a large and powerful union.

During the 1930s, car makers were hostile to unions and sometimes used violence against union members and organizers. Reuther guided the UAW though such conflicts, and won large wage hikes and important benefits from the companies.

As a young man, Reuther went to the Soviet Union and saw the lack of freedom there firsthand. After that, he became a strong enemy of communism in U.S. labor unions. He also fought against union bosses who set themselves up as dictators and did little to help their workers.

Paul Revere
American Patriot
1735-1818

Paul Revere's dramatic horseback ride on the night of April 18, 1775, is an important event in American history. Revere, a silversmith from Boston, rode through the Massachusetts countryside, warning people that British troops were coming. The troops had been sent to arrest rebel leaders and to destroy all guns and supplies. The rebels were American colonists opposed to the high taxes and limited rights under British rule.

Revere was able to spread the warning as far as the town of Lexington, but a British patrol stopped him on his way to Concord. Another rider got through and warned American patriots there. The next day, rebels known as Minutemen fought British troops at Lexington and Concord—the first battles of the American Revolution (1775-1783).

Eddie Rickenbacker
World War I Flying Ace
1890-1973

Eddie Rickenbacker became a hero during World War I (1914-1918) by shooting down 22 enemy planes and four enemy balloons. That tally made him America's leading flying ace. (Only aviators who have shot down at least five planes can be called an ace.)

Rickenbacker launched a successful career in business after the war. During World War II, he helped U.S. armed forces as an adviser. On October 21, 1942, a plane that he was in was forced down in the Pacific Ocean. Rickenbacker and seven other men struggled to stay alive with almost no food or water. Rickenbacker and all but one of the others were rescued after 24 days at sea.

Sally Ride
First American Woman in Space
1951-

On June 18, 1983, Sally Ride became the first American woman to go into space. Her history-making flight took place on the space shuttle *Challenger*. During the six-day mission, the shuttle crew released communications satellites and did medical research.

Ride was not the first female astronaut. Two Russian women were sent into space during the 1960s. However, when the U.S. space program began in the late 1950s, it did not consider women as astronaut material. Ride's journey into space put an end to that discrimination. Since 1983, women have regularly flown on space shuttle missions.

Jacob Riis
Crusading Photographer
1849–1914

In the 1880s, Jacob Riis (rees) was a newspaper reporter in New York City. He wrote about crime and the horrible living conditions of poor people there. However, many readers thought that Riis was exaggerating how bad things were. So he learned photography to prove that he wasn't.

The photos in his 1890 book, *How The Other Half Lives*, showed ordinary Americans the brutal poverty in big cities. The shock this caused led to reforms in housing and schools. Millions of poor immigrants to the U.S. benefited from the changes that Riis helped bring about.

Paul Robeson
Singer and Political Activist
1898–1976

As a young man, Paul Robeson (ROBE-sun) did everything well. He was a top-notch football player and earned a law degree at a time when most African Americans never made it through high school.

In the 1920s, Robeson became the most celebrated black actor and singer in the U.S. He captivated audiences in such plays as *The Emperor Jones* and *Othello*. His powerful version of the song "Ol' Man River," from the musical *Show Boat*, made it a classic.

In the 1950s, Robeson's ties to the Communist Party ruined his career. He was banned from performing in the United States and forced to move to Europe. He finally returned to the U.S. in 1963.

Robespierre
French Revolution Leader
1758-1794

Maximilien-François-Marie-Isidore de Robespierre (ROHBZ-pee-AIR) began his political career as a passionate believer in freedom and democracy. He became a leader in the French Revolution, which began in 1789 and lasted 10 years.

As the revolution progressed, however, Robespierre turned radical. He called for the execution of France's King Louis XVI, and his demand was granted in 1792. As his power increased, he and his allies created a "Reign of Terror." Anyone who criticized the revolution was beheaded by guillotine, an executioners' device that dropped a sharp, heavy blade.

During the Terror, at least 17,000 people were executed. Finally, people became tired of Robespierre's dictatorship and he himself was guillotined. The Terror ended soon afterward.

Jackie Robinson
First Black Player in Major-league Baseball
1919-1972

Sugar Ray Robinson
Boxing Champion
1921-1989

THIS GUY HITS HARD!

Sugar Ray Robinson was born Walker Smith in Ailey, Georgia. He got the name Ray Robinson after he used the certificate of another boxer to qualify for a fight. He became *Sugar* Ray because one sportswriter called his style in the ring "sweet as sugar."

Robinson is the only boxer to win the middle-weight title five times. He retired in 1965 with a record of 175 victories in 202 pro-fessional fights. Most of his losses came after he had turned 40. Pound for pound, many experts consider Robinson to be the greatest boxer ever.

In 1947, Jackie Robinson became the first African American to play major-league baseball when he was signed by Branch Rickey, general manager of the Brooklyn (now Los Angeles) Dodgers. Robinson's appearance on the baseball diamond sent shock waves through the entire U.S. At the time, the country was sharply divided along racial lines, and whites and blacks played in separate leagues.

Jack Roosevelt Robinson faced many obstacles. He was taunted by fans, opposing players, and even teammates. He also received death threats. However, he performed brilliantly. In 1947, he was named Rookie of the Year, and he retired in 1956 with a lifetime batting average of .311. In 1962, Robinson became the first African American elected to the National Baseball Hall of Fame.

John D. Rockefeller
Oil Millionaire
1839-1937

John D. Rockefeller spent the first part of his life building a business empire. Using practices that were often unfair, he seized control of the entire U.S. oil industry. His monopoly on oil gave him a vast fortune that would be worth $190 billion today. Such monopolies were later broken up by U.S. courts. Rockefeller spent the second part of his life giving away hundreds of millions of dollars to charity.

Rockefeller's family still has a high profile in the U.S. One of his grandsons, Nelson Rockefeller (1908-1979), served as New York's governor and vice president of the United States. Several other Rockefellers have held high positions in business and government.

Norman Rockwell
Artist
1894-1978

For most of the 1900s, Norman Rockwell *(left)* was the best-known artist in the U.S. His illustrations graced the covers of popular magazines such as *The Saturday Evening Post* and *Boys' Life*. During World War II, Rockwell did a series of patriotic paintings called "The Four Freedoms" that were widely distributed.

Rockwell's paintings showed great attention to detail as well as gentleness, warmth, and humor. Many art critics said that they gave a corny, overly romantic view of American life. Books of Rockwell's painting always sold well, but lately there has been a new appreciation of his work, and his paintings now sell for record prices.

Auguste Rodin
Sculptor
1840-1917

Auguste Rodin *(oh-GOOST ROH-dahn)* is considered the greatest sculptor of the late 1800s and early 1900s. He created some of the most famous of all sculptures, including *The Thinker*—a seated man, deep in thought, resting his chin on his hand.

Rodin's work was not appreciated early in his career. He supported himself by making ornaments for businesses. In time, however, people recognized his talent. Today, many of his works can be found in museums in the U.S. and France.

QUIET! I'M THINKING!

John Augustus Roebling
Builder of the Brooklyn Bridge
1806-1869

John Augustus Roebling *(ROE-bling)* designed New York City's Brooklyn Bridge, considered "the eighth wonder of the world" when it was completed in 1883. The 1,595-foot-long bridge connected Manhattan and Brooklyn. At that time, it was the largest suspension bridge ever built. A suspension bridge uses massive steel cables to support the weight of traffic.

Roebling pioneered the construction of suspension bridges, building three others around the country. He died in an accident before the Brooklyn Bridge could be finished. His son Washington Roebling, and Washington's wife, Emily, overcame great obstacles to carry out John Roebling's vision for the Brooklyn Bridge.

WILL ROGERS
HUMORIST
1879-1935

Eleanor Roosevelt
First Lady and Humanitarian
1884-1962

Eleanor Roosevelt *(ROH-zuh-velt)* was the wife of President Franklin Roosevelt, who held office from 1933 until his death in 1945. Franklin was crippled by polio, so Eleanor often served as his eyes and ears, going places that he could not. She was also a highly educated, strong-minded woman who fervently believed in helping the underprivileged. Her outspoken support for controversial causes, such as racial equality and improved labor conditions, made her both widely loved and widely hated.

After her husband's death, Eleanor Roosevelt was named a delegate to the United Nations (UN). She was key in writing the Universal Declaration of Human Rights, which the U.N. approved in 1948.

In the early 1900s, Will Rogers was America's most famous humorist. He became a Broadway star in 1916 using an act that combined rope tricks with homespun humor. Rogers joked about issues of the day, and his line, "All I know is what I read in the papers," was often repeated by fans.

Rogers, who was born in Oklahoma, was proud to be part Cherokee Indian. He appeared in 71 movies and wrote a column that ran in 350 newspapers. At age 55, he died in a plane crash. Although Rogers poked gentle fun at many people, he is best remembered for saying, "I never met a man I didn't like."

Franklin D. Roosevelt
32nd U.S. President
1882-1945

Franklin D. Roosevelt *(ROH-zuh-velt)* is often considered the greatest U.S. president of the 20th century. He guided the country though two of its biggest crises— the Great Depression (1929-1940) and World War II (1939-1945).

The Great Depression was a worldwide economic collapse. During that time, about one quarter of all Americans lost their jobs. Roosevelt was elected president in 1932, during the worst days of the Depression. His optimism and helpful government programs gave people hope.

During World War II, the U.S. and its allies fought Nazi Germany, Japan, and their allies. Roosevelt's steady leadership led the U.S. through many dark, uncertain months. He served in office for 12 years, longer than any other U.S. president.

Theodore Roosevelt
U.S. President
1858-1919

In 1900, Theodore Roosevelt (*ROH-zuh-velt*) was elected vice president on the Republican ticket with President William McKinley. In 1901, McKinley was assassinated and Roosevelt took over. He was the youngest person ever sworn in as U.S. president.

Roosevelt greatly expanded the powers of the president. He stopped companies from fixing prices, added millions of acres to the National Parks system, and launched the Panama Canal. In 1906, he became the first American to win a Nobel Peace Prize—for settling a war between Russia and Japan.

People loved Roosevelt's outgoing ways and called him "Teddy" or "T.R." When a cartoonist showed him as a hunter refusing to shoot a bear cub, it started a craze for new stuffed toys called "teddy bears." He left office in 1909.

Nellie Tayloe Ross
First Female Governor
1876~1977

Montana

Wyoming

North Dakota

Idaho

South Dakota

Utah

In 1925, Nellie Tayloe Ross became the governor of Wyoming—the first woman to ever become governor of a state. She was elected in 1924 to take over from her husband, William B. Ross, who had been governor and had died in office that year.

Ross, a Democrat, was defeated two years later in her bid for reelection. In 1933, President Franklin Roosevelt made her director of the U.S. Mint, the agency that issues the country's money. She was the first woman to hold that job as well. She also held high offices in the Democratic Party at a time when few women did so.

Jean-Jacques Rousseau
Philosopher
1712-1782

Jean-Jacques Rousseau (*jhahn-zhahk ruh-SOH*) was one of the most important philosophers of the European Enlightenment, a period that lasted from the late 1600s to the late 1700s.

Rousseau, a strong believer in democracy, said that laws are not binding unless people agree to them. This idea was radical for its time and greatly influenced the French Revolution (1789-1799).

Rousseau also believed that science, art, and society had corrupted humans and made them cruel. He believed that people should live as simple farmers instead. Among his most famous works are *The Social Contract* and *Confessions*.

Wilma Rudolph
Olympic Champion
1940-1994

During the 1960 Olympic Games in Rome, Wilma Rudolph became the first U.S. woman to win three gold medals in track and field. Rudolph won them in the 100-meter and 200-meter races. She also helped lead the 400-meter relay team to victory.

At age 4, Rudolph was struck by a series of illnesses, including polio. They left her unable to walk normally until she was 11. Despite these handicaps, she became a star basketball player and competed in her first Olympics when she was just 16. Later in life, Rudolph became a teacher and coach.

Bertrand Russell
Mathematician and Philosopher
1872-1970

Bertrand Russell is one of the most brilliant philosophers of the 20th century. In 1913, Russell and a co-author wrote a complex book called *Principia Mathematica*. It revolutionized both math and the study of logic.

Russell also wrote dozens of other important books on science, education, history, religion, and politics. A well-known atheist (someone who does not believe in God), he spoke out strongly against Christianity. He was also a pacifist—someone opposed to all fighting. He was imprisoned during World War I (1914-1918) for his antiwar views and again in the 1960s for his actions protesting the war in Vietnam.

Russell had a clear, direct writing style that critics praised. In 1950, he won the Nobel Prize for literature.

Bill Russell
Basketball Star
1934-

Bill Russell was the finest defensive player in pro basketball history. At 6 feet, 10 inches tall, Russell played center, and he could block shots or grab rebounds better than any competitor. Only Wilt Chamberlain is considered a rival for the title of the best all-around center.

During Russell's 13-year career, he led the Boston Celtics to 11 National Basketball Association (NBA) championships. He was voted the NBA's Most Valuable Player five times. From 1966 to 1969, Russell served as both a player and head coach. That made him the first African American to coach any professional sports team.

Babe Ruth
Major-league Slugger
1895-1948

In 1920, the Boston Red Sox sold outfielder (and former pitcher) George Herman "Babe" Ruth to the New York Yankees for $125,000. It was a huge mistake. As a Yankee, Ruth set every home-run record in baseball. His 1927 record for most home runs in a single season (60) stood until 1961. His career home-run record (714) remained unbroken until 1974. "The Sultan of Swat" played in 10 World Series—8 with Boston and 2 with New York—and set several records for both hitting and pitching.

Yankee Stadium is still known as "the House that Ruth Built." In 1936, Ruth became one of the first five players elected to the National Baseball Hall of Fame.

Nolan Ryan
Pitching Ace
1947-

Nolan Ryan is major-league baseball's all-time strikeout leader. On August 22, 1989, the Texas Rangers right-hander became the first pitcher to reach the 5,000-strikeout mark. It was an amazing accomplishment given that Ryan was 42, much older than most other players.

Ryan first began playing pro baseball in 1966. He pitched for several teams, including the New York Mets and the California Angels. In 1973, he set the record for the most strike-outs in a season with 383. In 1991, he pitched his seventh no-hitter, another record. Ryan won more than 300 games during his career, which ended in 1993.

Albert Sabin
1906-1993

Jonas Salk
1914-1995

The Men Who Conquered Polio

In the first half of the 20th century, polio was one of the most dreaded diseases in the world. It struck rich and poor alike, and killed millions of people. It left others horribly crippled.

Fear of the polio virus sparked a fierce competition among scientists. They wanted to find a vaccine that would stop the disease. A vaccine is a weakened version of a virus. It helps a body get used to, then resist, a disease without making the person sick.

In 1955, Jonas Salk won the race. His vaccine caused polio rates to drop. However, it had to be injected, which was painful, and it lasted only a few years. In 1961, Albert Sabin (SAY-bin) introduced a vaccine that could be placed in a sugar cube, so children could swallow it easily, and that gave lifelong protection. Though Sabin's vaccine is the one most commonly used today, both men saved millions of lives.

SACAGAWEA
EXPLORER AND GUIDE
ABOUT 1787-1812 OR 1814

Sacagawea (SAK-uh-juh-WEE-uh) was a young Indian woman who accompanied Lewis and Clark on their 1805-1806 journey to explore the west. She was a Shoshone Indian who had been captured by a rival tribe and sold to a French trapper. The trapper was hired by Lewis and Clark, and Sacagawea—carrying her infant child—went along.

Sacagawea, whose name means "Bird Woman," helped make the expedition successful. She served as an interpreter, obtained horses, identified plants and animals, and smoothed over tensions with Indian tribes. When a boat tipped over, she saved valuable journals and records. Both Lewis and Clark admired her strength and bravery.

Anwar el-Sadat
Statesman
1918-1981

EGYPT

Nile River

EGYPT

Red Sea

Africa

As president of Egypt, Anwar el-Sadat *(AHN-wahr el-suh-DAHT)* helped end his country's long-time conflict with Israel. In 1977, Sadat visited Israel, a mostly Jewish country, and kicked off a series of negotiations. Eventually, they led to a peace treaty between the two countries. Sadat was widely praised in the U.S. and Europe, and was co-winner of the 1978 Nobel Peace Prize.

However, the peace treaty made Sadat very unpopular with many Egyptians, most of whom are Muslim. Dissatisfaction with Sadat grew more intense because he mismanaged Egypt's economy and banned public criticism. He ruled as president from 1970 until 1981, when he was assassinated by Muslim radicals.

Carl Sagan
Astronomer and
Best-selling Author
1934-1996

Carl Sagan *(SAY-gun)* was a scientist who became famous for being able to explain difficult subjects to ordinary people. Sagan believed that people need to understand science better, because our lives are dominated by technology. He also believed that science helps improve critical thinking, a skill that people use to decide what is true and untrue.

Sagan's best-known work was the 1980 television series *Cosmos*, which helped viewers "see" and explore outer space. He also wrote several popular science books. In 1977, he won a Pulitzer Prize for *The Dragons of Eden*. His other books include *Bronca's Brain* and *The Demon-Haunted World: Science as a Candle in the Dark*.

Margaret Sanger
Social Reformer
1879-1966

Margaret Sanger launched the movement to legalize birth control in the U.S. In the early 1900s, it was illegal for most doctors to mention birth-control methods to their patients. It was also illegal to send birth-control information through the mail, because it was considered obscene.

Sanger, a nurse, was a strong believer in women's rights. She saw how unwanted pregnancies could ruin lives. In 1917, she was imprisoned for running a birth-control clinic in New York. Sanger went to court to challenge the bans on birth-control information, and won. She also founded Planned Parenthood, a group that promotes health care for women and families as well as birth control.

Antonio López de Santa Anna
Dictator
1795-1876

Antonio López de Santa Anna (*SAHN-tuh AH-nuh*) became president of Mexico no fewer than 11 times between 1833 and 1853. A ruthless dictator, he was overthrown each time.

Santa Anna's rule was disastrous for Mexico. In the 1830s, his high-handed ways prompted Texas to revolt. Santa Anna led the forces that captured the Alamo and massacred its defenders in 1836. Later that year, Santa Anna was defeated by forces led by American Sam Houston, and Texas became independent.

Santa Anna also led his country during the Mexican-American War (1846-1848). He was badly defeated once again, and Mexico lost huge sections of its territory to the U.S. He died penniless in Mexico City, Mexico.

Franz Schubert
Composer
1797-1828

Franz Schubert *(SHOO-burt)* was a musical genius. He began composing when he was only 13, and he was still a teenager when he wrote some of his most famous short compositions.

Schubert tried to write operas to earn money. However, they were never performed. He also wrote symphonies, but few of them made it to the concert hall. As a result, Schubert remained poor and received little recognition during his brief 31-year life. However, he was a master of writing short pieces—he composed eight of them in one day. His famous works include *Symphony in C Major* and "The Trout" quintet.

Charles M. Schulz
Creator of the *Peanuts* Cartoon
1922-2000

For 50 years, cartoonist Charles M. Schulz drew *Peanuts*, the most beloved comic strip in the world. It appeared in 2,000 newspapers in more than 70 countries. Schulz's strip was the basis for several television specials, as well as for a Broadway musical called *You're a Good Man, Charlie Brown*.

The strip had many well-known characters, including Snoopy, Lucy, and Linus, but Charlie Brown was the main character. He was a bland but good-hearted child who was often the butt of other kids' jokes. *Peanuts* readers sympathized with his problems and enjoyed the strip's simple wisdom.

Albert Schweitzer
Philosopher and Humanitarian
1875-1965

By the time he was 30, Albert Schweitzer (*SHWYT-sur*) was a famous religious and musical scholar. In 1913, he earned a medical degree, then left his homeland (then part of Germany, now of France). He went to Africa, to what today is the country of Gabon, and set up a hospital in the jungle. Thousands of poor Africans were treated there each year.

While running the hospital, Schweitzer continued to write important books, including *The Philosophy of Civilization* and *Out of My Life and Thought*. His deep religious faith and self-sacrifice earned him worldwide respect. He won many awards, including the 1952 Nobel Peace Prize for his work toward "the Brotherhood of Nations."

Dred Scott
Famous American Slave
1795-1858

In the 1850s, Dred Scott was the slave of a master who lived in Missouri, a state that allowed slavery. However, Scott's master took his slave with him when he moved to Illinois, then to Wisconsin Territory, two places where slavery had been banned. Later, they moved back to Missouri. Scott sued his master, saying that since he had lived in a free state, he should be a free man.

In 1857, the U.S. Supreme Court ruled against Scott. It declared that no black person— free or slave—could become a U.S. citizen. This ruling outraged the North and helped lead to the outbreak of the U.S. Civil War (1861-1965). Dred Scott won his freedom shortly after the ruling.

MAURICE SENDAK
CHILDREN'S BOOK AUTHOR AND ILLUSTRATOR
1928-

Millions of children have gone to sleep after hearing a parent read *Where the Wild Things Are*. That book was the brainchild of writer and artist Maurice Sendak. He won the 1964 Caldecott Medal for its beautiful illustrations.

Sendak, the son of Polish immigrants, began his art career by doing illustrations for comic books and toy-store windows. He did the art for more than 80 children's books by other writers before writing and illustrating his own. Sendak's most popular books include *Kenny's Window*, *In the Night Kitchen*, and *Really Rosie*, which was made into a television special.

153

Seneca the Younger
Writer and Statesman of Ancient Rome
4 B.C.–A.D. 65

Seneca the Younger was one of the most talented men in Roman history. His father, Seneca the Elder, was a famous politician and author.

Seneca the Younger entered politics as well. In 54 A.D., he was named chief adviser to the emperor Nero, whom he had tutored earlier. Seneca introduced reforms to the government that greatly improved Rome. Over time, though, Nero became murderous and unstable. To save his own life, Seneca retired to his country home. Nero still mistrusted him, however, and eventually ordered him to take his own life.

In his last years, Seneca wrote several important works on philosophy that are still being read today.

SEQUOYAH
INVENTOR OF THE CHEROKEE ALPHABET
1760-1843

Sequoyah (sih-KWOY-uh) was a Cherokee Indian who believed that European settlers were powerful because of their written language. He saw that writing allowed them to collect and spread more information than the Cherokees, whose language was only spoken. After 12 years of struggle, Sequoyah created a written alphabet for the Cherokee language. It used 86 symbols. Introduced in 1821, the alphabet quickly caught on with the Cherokee, and was used in books, magazines and newspapers.

The sequoia, a type of giant redwood tree that grows along the Pacific Coast, was named for the great inventor.

Junípero Serra
Apostle of California
1713-1784

Junípero Serra (hoo-NEE-puh-roh SEHR-uh) was a Roman Catholic priest from Spain who helped to settle California and spread Christianity. In 1769, Serra founded Mission San Diego near the present-day city of San Diego. In time, he established eight more missions in California. Their goal was to promote Spanish power and to convert Indians to Christianity.

Serra's work earned him the title "Apostle of California." (An *apostle* is someone who spreads the teachings of a religious leader or philosopher.) Since 1934, many Roman Catholics have tried to have Serra declared a saint. However, Native Americans say that his missions enslaved their ancestors and destroyed their culture. Serra's defenders say that he was a good friend to California Indians.

Dr. Seuss
Children's Book Author and Illustrator
1904-1991

Dr. Seuss *(soos)* may be the most famous children's book author and illustrator of the 20th century. His more than 50 books combine funny cartoons with silly poems that should not make sense, but do anyway. Seuss's books are known for being able to teach children how to read while entertaining them at the same time.

Dr. Seuss was the pen name of Theodor Seuss Geisel *(GYE-zul)*. He wrote and illustrated his first children's book in 1937. He went on to create such classics as *The Cat in the Hat, Horton Hears a Who, Green Eggs and Ham,* and *How the Grinch Stole Christmas*. In 1984, Dr. Seuss was awarded a special Pulitzer Prize for his work.

William Shakespeare
The World's Greatest Playwright
1564-1616

As a writer, William Shakespeare is in a league by himself. Today, nearly four centuries after his death, plays that he wrote—such as *Romeo and Juliet, Othello,* and *Twelfth Night*—are still produced all over the world. Many have been made into movies. Both his plays and his poetry are considered the best in the English language.

Shakespeare's greatest talent was probably his ability to create lifelike, complex characters. His villains—Macbeth, for instance—have good qualities as well as bad, and they struggle over the evil that they do. His heroes, such as Hamlet, are often unsure how to do the right thing.

Shakespeare wrote 37 plays in all—hilarious comedies as well as moving tragedies. All carry tremendous power. He is also famous for his sonnets, a form of poetry.

Scenes from some of William Shakespeare's most famous plays:

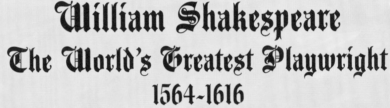

Othello

A Midsummer Night's Dream

Romeo and Juliet

Much Ado About Nothing

Hamlet

The Tempest

Julius Caesar

George Bernard Shaw
Playwright
1856-1950

George Bernard Shaw became one of Great Britain's most famous playwrights. As a young man, however, he endured great poverty while trying to become a writer.

Shaw's novels flopped, so he turned to writing plays. He created plays to make a point rather than to tell a story. Most of them focused on the phoniness and unfairness in English society.

Shaw, who was born and raised in Ireland, wrote several still-famous plays, such as *Arms and the Man*, *Man and Superman*, and *Saint Joan*. The comedy *Pygmalion* is probably his best-known play. It later was adapted into a musical called *My Fair Lady*. Shaw won the 1925 Nobel Prize for literature.

Mary Shelley
Creator of *Frankenstein*
1797-1851

Mary Shelley was an English novelist who is best remembered for writing *Frankenstein*. The 1818 novel is a tragedy about a scientist who artificially creates a monstrous-looking human being. Shelley's book later became the basis for several horror movies.

In the book, a scientist struggles with the unexpected results of creating a new kind of creature. Recent breakthroughs have enabled scientists to clone animals and to change plants and animals in other ways. As experts debate the possible results of such advances, the theme of *Frankenstein* remains fresh.

Mary Shelley was the wife of Percy Bysshe Shelley, a famous English poet. When he drowned in 1822, she wrote other novels to support her family. None became as popular as *Frankenstein*.

Alan B. Shepard Jr.
First American in Space
1923-1998

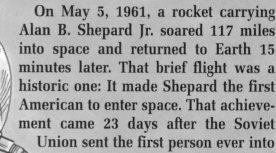

On May 5, 1961, a rocket carrying Alan B. Shepard Jr. soared 117 miles into space and returned to Earth 15 minutes later. That brief flight was a historic one: It made Shepard the first American to enter space. That achievement came 23 days after the Soviet Union sent the first person ever into space. At the time, the U.S. and the Soviet Union were locked in a "space race." Both sides wanted to reach the moon first. The U.S. won that race in 1969.

In 1971, Shepard commanded the *Apollo 14* mission and became the fifth man to walk on the moon.

Shih Huangdi
First Emperor of Unified China
259 B.C.-210 B.C.

In 221 B.C., Shih Huangdi (*shihr hwahng-dee*) united China's warring territories under one government for the first time. Born Chao Cheng, he took on the title Shih Huangdi, which means "First Sovereign Emperor."

Shih Huangdi founded the Qin dynasty (ruling family), which he believed would control China for 10,000 years. Instead, it collapsed only four years after his death. That is largely because Shih Huangdi was a brutal emperor who killed opponents, burned their books, and mistrusted everyone. However, he also greatly improved China's government and had the Great Wall of China built.

Ol' Blue Eyes

The Voice

Chairman of the Board

Frank Sinatra
Singer and Movie Star
1915-1998

The first teen singing idol was not Elvis Presley or the Beatles. It was Frank Sinatra. In the early 1940s, teenage girls called "bobby-soxers" screamed and cried at the sight of the slim, young crooner they called "The Voice."

Sinatra expanded into movies. In 1953, he won an Academy Award for best supporting actor in *From Here to Eternity*. In all, he appeared in more than 50 films.

However, it was Sinatra's singing that made him famous and kept him famous. Some of his biggest hits include "Strangers in the Night," "My Way," and "New York, New York." Sinatra won nine Grammy awards, sold millions of records, and established a pop singing style that has influenced countless musicians and singers.

SITTING BULL
SIOUX
INDIAN LEADER
1834-1890

As a boy, Sitting Bull was called "Slow." After showing bravery in battle, however, he earned the name Sitting Bull. In time, he became leader of the entire Sioux nation.

As a medicine man, Sitting Bull had visions of victory over the U.S. Army. These visions encouraged the Sioux and other Indians to wipe out the forces of Lieutenant Colonel George Armstrong Custer at the Battle of Little Big Horn in 1876.

Sitting Bull was finally defeated and forced to live on a reservation. For a while, he toured with Buffalo Bill's Wild West show. He was killed in a dispute with Indian police.

Socrates
Philosopher of Ancient Greece
469-399 B.C.

Socrates (*SAHK-ruh-teez*) is considered the greatest philosopher of the ancient world. He prowled the streets of his hometown, Athens, seeking out conversations with the most intelligent people.

Socrates liked to discuss issues, such as the nature of justice and morality. By questioning people, he found out what they truly knew and believed. This way of teaching—by asking repeated questions—is called the Socratic method.

Socrates was quick to point out the flaws of democracy as it existed in Athens. His criticisms finally led to a trial. Found guilty of corrupting the young and dishonoring the gods, he was given the death penalty. He had to drink hemlock, a poison that killed him.

Sophocles
Playwright
496-406 B.C.

Sophocles (*SAHF-uh-kleez*) is one of three great tragic playwrights from ancient Greece. The other two are Aeschylus (*ESS-kuh-lus*) and Euripides (*yuh-RIP-uh-deez*). Sophocles wrote more than 120 plays, but only seven complete ones have survived. His two most famous plays are *Oedipus (EE-duh-pus) the King* and *Antigone (an-TIG-uh-nee)*.

In ancient Greece, plays were performed during competitions. Sophocles won more awards than any other playwright.

Sophocles made several important changes to the theater. He was the first writer to add a third character on stage. He also was the first to use painted scenery to show where the action was taking place.

John Philip Sousa
Composer and Bandleader
1854-1932

A-ONE AND A-TWO AND . . .

Marching bands everywhere owe a debt to John Philip Sousa (*SOO-zuh*). He is known as the "March King" because he wrote so many famous marching songs, including "The Stars and Stripes Forever" and "The Washington Post."

In 1880, Sousa became leader of the U.S. Marine Band. He shaped it into a world-class musical group.

Sousa wrote different kinds of music, including waltzes and operettas. Many of those works became popular. However, Sousa's fame rests on his 140 marches. Other composers have written marches, but Sousa's tunes have a special energy and rousing spirit that make them unforgettable. He remains one of America's most famous composers.

Spartacus
Leader of Roman Slave Revolt
Unknown–71 B.C.

Steven Spielberg
Director of Hollywood Blockbusters
1947–

Mark Spitz
Olympic Champion
1950–

We know very little about Spartacus except that he led a slave rebellion that terrified ancient Rome. He was born in Greece and served in the Roman army for a time. When Spartacus left the army without permission, he was captured and forced to become a gladiator. Gladiators were slaves who had to fight other gladiators to the death, to entertain crowds of bloodthirsty spectators.

In 73 B.C., Spartacus began a slave revolt. Thousands of other slaves rushed to join him. With an army of more than 70,000 escaped slaves, Spartacus crushed one Roman army after another. In 71 B.C., however, he finally lost. He was killed in battle and his followers were executed.

In 1975, director Steven Spielberg scared the wits out of moviegoers with *Jaws*, a film about a killer shark. He then went on to direct and write some of the biggest blockbusters in Hollywood history, including *Close Encounters of the Third Kind*, *E.T.: The Extra-Terrestrial*, and *Jurassic Park*, as well as *Raiders of the Lost Ark* and the two other Indiana Jones movies.

Until the 1990s, Spielberg was known mainly for making crowd-pleasing action and adventure movies. However, in 1993, he directed *Schindler's List*, a moving and difficult film about the Holocaust. The movie had a huge impact on audiences, and Spielberg was given an Academy Award for best director.

Mark Spitz was the first athlete to win seven gold medals at a single Olympics. In 1972, he came in first in all seven of the swimming events that he entered at the Munich Olympic Games. The U.S. swim-team star also set world records in those events.

Four years earlier, at the 1968 Olympics in Mexico City, Spitz had won four medals: two golds, one silver, and one bronze. That performance was a letdown, however, because Spitz had predicted that he would win six gold medals that year. In 1972, he finally made good on his prediction—and became a world-famous athlete.

Mark Spitz is tied with Carl Lewis, U.S. track star, for winning the most Olympic gold medals overall: Each has a lifetime total of nine.

BENJAMIN SPOCK
BABY-CARE SPECIALIST
1903-1998

In 1946, Benjamin Spock, a New York baby doctor, published a book called *Common Sense Book of Baby and Child Care*. It hit the stores just as the U.S. was going through a "baby boom" (a period of time, after World War II, when more babies were born than usual). Spock's book became a runaway best-seller, and influenced several generations of parents.

THAT'S MY DOC!

Spock wrote his book because he disagreed with the rigid, uncaring advice that many baby doctors had previously given out. Some of those doctors accused Spock of being too easygoing with children. In the 1960s and 1970s, Spock became even more controversial by speaking out strongly against U.S. involvement in the Vietnam War (1965-1973).

JOSEPH STALIN
SOVIET DICTATOR
1879-1953

Joseph Stalin *(STAHL-un)* was one of the cruelest, most powerful dictators in history. He rose to power as an associate of Lenin in the Russian revolution of 1917. After Lenin's death in 1924, Stalin seized control of the government, ruthlessly wiping out his rivals.

Stalin's communist policies changed the Soviet Union from a backward farming country into a world power. However, those forceful, often-harsh policies led to great suffering for the Soviet people.

Stalin directed the Russian military in World War II (1939-1945), helping to defeat Germany. Later, his control spread through Eastern Europe and led to the Cold War (1946-1989), a time of tense relations between his country and the U.S. By the time Stalin died in 1953, he had enslaved or murdered millions of people.

Elizabeth Cady Stanton
Pioneer for Women's Rights
1815-1902

Elizabeth Cady Stanton was one of the Founding Mothers of the women's rights movement. She was highly educated, and learned about women's inequality while studying in her father's law office.

Stanton helped organize the first women's-rights convention, which took place in 1848 in Seneca Falls, New York. The male-run newspapers of the time made fun of the convention's goals, which included giving women the right to own property and the right to vote.

For the rest of her life, Stanton campaigned tirelessly to improve women's lives. She scored many victories. The biggest came after her death: In 1920, U.S. women finally won the right to vote.

Robert Louis Stevenson
Novelist
1850-1894

Any child who ever dreamed of adventure has longed to live in the books of Robert Louis Stevenson. He wrote *Treasure Island* and *Kidnapped*, two of the greatest young people's action novels of all time.

Stevenson also wrote a hugely popular horror novel, *The Strange Case of Dr. Jekyll and Mr. Hyde*. It is a brilliant study of the good and evil in all people. He was a skilled essayist and poet as well. His book *A Child's Garden of Verses* is a well-loved classic.

Stevenson, born in Scotland, was sickly as a child and young adult. He moved to a South Pacific island for his health. His kindness and generosity won him many friends there. People of the island built a road to his house and called it the "Road of the Loving Heart."

I'M MR. HYDE. HAVE YOU SEEN DR. JEKYLL?

SAY CHEESE!

ALFRED STIEGLITZ
PHOTOGRAPHER
1864-1946

Alfred Stieglitz (STEEG-lits) helped turn photography into an art form. In the late 1800s, photographers were looked down on by painters, sculptors, and other artists. They believed that a picture taken by a camera, which was a mechanical device, could not compare with artwork done by hand.

Stieglitz spent his life changing that idea. He persuaded museums and art galleries to put photographs on their walls. He also worked hard to take striking pictures. He once spent three hours in a New York blizzard to capture a street scene just right. That photograph, called *Fifth Avenue, Winter*, is now considered a work of art.

Lucy Stone
Women's-rights Pioneer
1818-1893

Lucy Stone was probably the first married woman in the U.S. to keep her maiden name. In 1855, when she married a merchant named Henry Blackwell, they agreed to treat each other as equals. Keeping her own name was part of that agreement. That may not seem unusual today, but it was shockingly radical at the time. Then, females were not considered capable of making important decisions. They went from having a father make decisions for them to having a husband do so.

In 1847, Stone became one of the first women in Massachusetts to graduate from college. She went on to become an outspoken foe of slavery. Later, she championed women's rights, especially the right to vote. In the late 1800s, a married woman who kept her maiden name was known as a "Lucy Stoner."

Harriet Beecher Stowe
Author of *Uncle Tom's Cabin*
1811-1896

In 1850, the sister of Connecticut-born Harriet Beecher Stowe challenged her to "write something that would make this whole nation feel what an accursed thing slavery is!" Stowe responded in 1852 with *Uncle Tom's Cabin; or, Life Among the Lowly.*

Stowe's novel, which showed the cruelties of slaves' lives, electrified the country. In the North, anti-slavery forces praised it as a work of genius. In the slave-holding South, it became dangerous for anyone to even own a copy. However, *Uncle Tom's Cabin* was a best-seller. Many historians count it as one of the causes of the U.S. Civil War (1961-1865).

Peter Stuyvesant
The Last Dutch Governor of New York
1610-1672

THEY'LL CALL IT "THE BIG APPLE" SOMEDAY!

If Peter Stuyvesant *(STY-vuh-sunt)* had been a better governor, New York City might have remained a Dutch colony. In 1647, Stuyvesant was put in control of New Amsterdam (now New York), and he quickly made enemies.

Stuyvesant refused all attempts to give Dutch colonists more say in their own government. Many of his policies were good, such as his peace treaties with local Indians. However, people hated his bossy, absolute rule.

In 1664, the English fleet sailed into New Amsterdam's harbor and ordered it to surrender. The city could have defended itself, but the Dutch colonists refused to fight. They preferred English rule over Stuyvesant's.

Suleiman I
Greatest Ottoman Emperor
1496~1566

Suleiman I *(SOO-lay-mahn)* was the most powerful ruler of the Ottoman Empire. The Ottomans came from what is now the country of Turkey. During Suleiman's reign, the Ottoman Empire was the richest, most-feared country in both Europe and the Middle East.

Suleiman (also spelled Süleyman) expanded his empire's borders in Europe, seizing control of Hungary and almost overrunning Austria. His naval fleets dominated the Mediterranean Sea. He also reformed the Ottoman legal code and increased trade with the Far East. Suleiman was called "the Magnificent" in Europe and "the Lawgiver" among his own people.

Sun Yat-Sen
Father of Modern China
1866-1925

CHINA

Sun Yat-Sen *(sun yaht-sen)* had three important goals: to overthrow China's Manchu rulers, to unify China, and to set up a strong republic. (A *republic* is a country where the people elect their government's leaders.) He succeeded in the first goal, but failed in the other two. Still, he is considered the man who started China on the road to modernization and power.

The Manchus, who had controlled China since 1644, fell from power in 1911. Sun set up a republic the next year, but he was too idealistic to be an effective politician. He was quickly ousted, and China experienced years of disorder. However, Sun's ideals helped guide his followers, who finally did unify China in the 1930s.

Ida M. Tarbell
Muckraking Journalist
1857-1944

The History of the Standard Oil Company by Ida M. Tarbell

In 1904, Ida M. Tarbell published *The History of the Standard Oil Company*. At that time, Standard Oil was probably the most powerful company in the world. Owned by John D. Rockefeller, it had become the sole source of oil for most Americans.

Tarbell's book showed the dishonest and unfair practices that Rockefeller used to create his oil empire. Her book helped lead to the breakup of Standard Oil's monopoly a few years later. Crusading journalists like Tarbell became known as "muckrakers." That is because they stirred up things that many powerful people preferred to leave alone.

Peter Ilich Tchaikovsky
Composer
1840-1893

Christmas would not be Christmas without Peter Ilich Tchaikovsky's *(chy-KAWF-skee)* ballet, *The Nutcracker*. In many places around the world, that ballet is performed every Christmas, and its music is as familiar at that time of year as popular Christmas carols. Tchaikovsky also created the music for two other well-known ballets, *Swan Lake* and *Sleeping Beauty*. They were just part of a huge body of work that shows his genius.

Tchaikovsky began life as a clerk in the Russian government, but soon threw himself into music. He became the best-known Russian composer in the world, writing dozens of symphonies and songs that are still played today.

A mystery surrounds Tchaikovsky's death: He may have died from disease, but some researchers suspect that he committed suicide.

Tecumseh
Shawnee Indian Leader
1765-1813

In the late 1700s, white settlers pushed westward into the territory that today is Ohio, Kentucky, Tennessee, Indiana, and Alabama. As that happened, Native Americans who lived in those areas suffered. Tecumseh *(tuh-KUM-suh)* saw many fellow Indians killed or driven off their land.

Tecumseh grew up to be a powerful warrior and speaker. He used both skills to build a strong Indian resistance to the white settlers. He hoped to create a strong union of Indian tribes, similar to the U.S. model of united states. Several tribes heeded his call to return to their traditional ways. They also fought settlers' efforts to steal their land. However, after Tecumseh died in a battle with U.S. Army troops, his efforts to unify the tribes collapsed.

Shirley Temple
Child Movie Star
1928-

When Shirley Temple was just six years old, she became the highest-paid movie star in Hollywood. Throughout the 1930s, fans flocked to see her in such movies as *Little Miss Marker*, *Wee Willie Winkie*, *Heidi*, and *Rebecca of Sunnybrook Farm*. Temple's glowing smile, dimpled cheeks, and famous curls were part of her appeal. She was also a gifted singer and dancer.

Temple's popularity faded as she entered her teenage years. By 1950, she had married and retired from making movies. In her adult years, she is known by her married name, Shirley Temple Black. Black has served as a U.S. ambassador and as a United Nations (UN) delegate.

Mother Teresa
Humanitarian
1910-1997

In 1950, a Roman Catholic nun named Mother Teresa founded a new religious order, called Missionaries of Charity. The order's task was to help poor people in Calcutta, India, one of the largest and most crowded cities on Earth.

Missionaries of Charity set up schools and treatment centers for the blind. They also established shelters where poor people who are very sick can die with dignity.

In 1979, Mother Teresa was awarded the Nobel Peace Prize for her compassionate work. Over time, her order expanded to 90 countries. About 4,000 nuns and hundreds of thousands of volunteers continue to minister to the poor, the sick, and the dying.

Valentina Tereshkova
First Woman in Space
1937-

On June 16, 1963, the Soviet Union's *Vostok 6* spacecraft soared into space. In it was Valentina Tereshkova *(vah-len-TEE-nuh ter-ush-KAW-vuh)*, the first female to travel in space.

Most cosmonauts had to be highly trained pilots before they were allowed to fly a spacecraft. Tereshkova was not. She was accepted by the Soviet space program because of her strong faith in communism and because she was an amateur parachute diver.

Tereshkova flew in *Vostok 6* around Earth 45 times for almost 71 hours. Once the spacecraft got close enough to Earth, she parachuted to safety. Tereshkova later became a powerful figure in the Soviet government.

Nikola Tesla
Pioneer in Electricity
1856-1943

The next time you plug in your radio or television, you can thank Nikola Tesla *(TESS-luh)*. He invented the alternating-current (AC) power system that brings electricity into homes and offices. In the U.S., among other countries, the AC system replaced the weaker direct-current (DC) system.

Tesla moved to the U.S. from Croatia in 1884. His first job was with Thomas Edison, but the two inventors did not get along. After splitting from Edison, Tesla developed the AC system, which competed directly with Edison's DC system. Tesla's system won out. He later laid the groundwork for the invention of radio and created a new system for lighting.

Henry David Thoreau
Writer and Philosopher
1817-1862

Henry David Thoreau *(thuh-ROH)* once wrote that "the mass of men lead lives of quiet desperation." He wanted to live differently, so he built a cabin in the woods near Walden Pond in Massachusetts. For two years, he lived there as simply as possible. Thoreau wrote his observations about life and nature in *Walden; or, Life in the Woods*. It became a classic book.

Thoreau also wrote *Civil Disobedience*, which said that people should peacefully disobey laws that are unjust. That essay greatly influenced Mohandas K. Gandhi and Martin Luther King Jr., who used civil disobedience in their political struggles for freedom and equal rights.

JIM THORPE
ATHLETE
1887-1953

Jim Thorpe was probably the greatest all-around athlete of the 20th century. At the 1912 Olympics in Oslo, Sweden, he won two gold medals, in the decathlon and pentathlon. "Sir, you are the greatest athlete in the world," the king of Sweden told Thorpe afterward.

At the time, the Olympics had a strict rule that athletes must be unpaid amateurs. In 1913, Olympic officials found out Thorpe had previously played semiprofessional baseball, so they stripped him of his medals. The medals were returned to Thorpe's family in 1983.

Thorpe, a Native American, was also a standout player in football, baseball, basketball, boxing, lacrosse, swimming, and hockey. The most valuable player award of the National Football League (NFL) is called the Jim Thorpe Trophy.

Thucydides
Historian
460-400 B.C.

Thucydides (*thoo-SID-uh-deez*) was the first historian whose goal was to write an unbiased account of past events. He wrote about the horrible war between Athens and Sparta that lasted from 431 to 404 B.C. Most of what we know about that event comes from Thucydides.

Along with Herodotus (*hih-ROD-uh-tuss*), Thucydides is considered the founder of history writing. Of the two historians, however, Thucydides was much more careful about how he gathered facts. He saw some of the war first-hand, as a soldier for Athens. He also interviewed people on both sides to get their views. Those methods are still used today by modern writers of history.

Hideki Tojo
Japanese Leader During World War II
1884-1948

Hideki Tojo (*hee-deh-kee TOH-joh*) was a general who led Japan's government during World War II (1939-1945). He was one of many generals who used murder and violence to take over Japan's government in the 1930s. Those generals then led the country to war against other countries in Asia, as well as the U.S.

Their goal was to create a vast empire in the Pacific Ocean. At first, it seemed as if they might succeed. By 1944, however, Japan was clearly losing and Tojo was forced from power. After the war, he was tried by the U.S. and its allies as a war criminal. He was found guilty and hanged.

Leo Tolstoy
Novelist
1828-1910

WAR AND PEACE

Leo Tolstoy (*tall-STOY*) wrote two of the greatest novels in history: *War and Peace* and *Anna Karenina*. The first is a story about five Russian families struggling through Napoleon's 1812 invasion of Russia. The second is about a wealthy woman who is unfaithful to her husband. It explores the cruelty and unfairness of Russian society.

Both are masterpieces because they show how people really think and feel. In 1879, Tolstoy (also spelled *Tolstoi*) had a religious conversion. He created his own brand of radical Christianity, which embraced simplicity and rejected all violence. Tolstoy kept writing, but his later work never matched his earlier masterpieces.

Harry S. Truman
33rd U.S. President
1882-1972

IN 1948, I HAD A BOWLING ALLEY BUILT IN THE BASEMENT OF THE WHITE HOUSE!

In 1945, in the closing months of World War II, President Franklin D. Roosevelt died suddenly. It fell to his vice president, Harry S. Truman, to guide the country through the war's end and the dangerous years afterward.

Perhaps Truman's biggest decision was to drop two atomic bombs on Japan. The bombs ended the war quickly, but they killed hundreds of thousands of people, most of whom were not soldiers involved in the fighting. Many people still debate whether Truman was correct.

In 1948, Truman, a Democrat, ran for reelection. He was unpopular, so few observers thought that he could win. He surprised them: Truman pulled off the greatest upset in presidential history by defeating Republican Thomas Dewey.

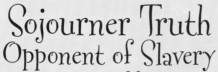

Sojourner Truth
Opponent of Slavery
1797-1883

Isabella Van Wagener lived as a slave in New York until 1827, when the state abolished slavery. In 1843, she heard God command her to speak out against slavery. She changed her name to Sojourner Truth and began preaching throughout the North.

Sojourner Truth was a spellbinding speaker who could draw huge crowds. She often began a speech by saying "Children, I talk to God, and God talks to me." In the 1850s, she started speaking for women's rights as well as against slavery.

Harriet Tubman
Conductor on the "Underground Railroad"
1820-1913

Harriet Tubman was the most famous "conductor" on the Underground Railroad. The "Railroad" was a network of people who helped African American slaves escape from their Southern masters before the U.S. Civil War (1861-1865).

Tubman herself escaped from slavery in 1849. She returned to the South 19 times and guided 300 slaves to freedom. She never lost a slave, partly because of her iron discipline. She promised to kill anyone who turned back.

In the South, rewards for Tubman's capture grew to $40,000. However, she was never caught. She went on to serve as a spy for the U.S. Army during the Civil War.

Nat Turner
Leader of a U.S. Slave Revolt
1800-1831

Nat Turner was a black slave and preacher who led the only effective slave revolt in U.S. history. In 1831, he and seven other slaves rebelled and marched toward what they hoped would be freedom. As they fled through the countryside, they and other slaves who joined them killed more than 60 whites.

Turner thought that thousands of slaves would join him, but only 75 did. He and his followers were soon captured and jailed, then killed. More than 100 innocent blacks were also killed.

Turner's uprising destroyed Southerners' belief that most blacks were happy to be slaves and that those who were not were too weak to fight back. To avoid other slave rebellions, Southern states soon passed laws that restricted the movement of blacks.

YOU CAN CALL ME TUT!

Tutankhamen
Pharaoh of Ancient Egypt
1300s B.C.

Tutankhamen *(too-tang-KAHM-un)* served as pharaoh, or king, of Egypt from about 1347 to 1339 B.C. He became king when he was about 9 and died when he was 18. Historians say that nothing special happened during his reign.

In 1922, though, King Tut—as he often is called today—suddenly became vital to our understanding of ancient Egypt. That is because Howard Carter, a British archaeologist, discovered Tut's tomb.

It marked the first and only time that scientists have found a pharaoh's tomb before grave robbers could pick it clean. The more than 5,000 objects found in Tut's tomb show the wealth and power of ancient Egypt. They also gave researchers valuable clues about life in that time and place.

Desmond Tutu
Human-rights Leader
1931-

Desmond Tutu became world-famous in 1984, when he was awarded the Nobel Peace Prize. It was given to him for his leadership in a peaceful struggle against the system of apartheid (separation of the races) in his homeland of South Africa. Although the majority of South Africans are black, whites controlled the government, the economy, and most other aspects of life.

Tutu, an Anglican minister, encouraged South Africans to use nonviolent actions to protest against their country's harsh racial laws. He also encouraged other countries to put economic pressure on South Africa to force it to change. In 1994, South Africa's white-ruled government finally fell—in part, because of Tutu's work. South Africa is now one of the leading democracies in Africa.

Mark Twain
Humorist and Writer
1835-1910

Huckleberry Finn

Tom Sawyer

As a young man, Mark Twain held two jobs that helped make him an outstanding writer late in life. He worked in a print shop, which taught him how to use language. Then he piloted a Mississippi riverboat, which gave him experiences that he put to use in write books set on the Mississippi River. Two such Twain books, *The Adventures of Tom Sawyer* and *Adventures of Huckleberry Finn*, are now classics. *The Prince and the Pauper* is another well-known Twain novel.

Twain's popularity came from his ability to make people laugh while saying important things about life. He was born Samuel Langhorne Clemens. His pen name, Mark Twain, came from a riverboat term that means "two fathoms deep"—a depth of about 12 feet.

Rudolph Valentino
Silent-movie Star
1895-1926

Rudolph Valentino was the greatest romantic leading man in silent movies. He moved to the U.S. from Italy in 1913 and changed his name, which was originally Rodolfo d'Antonguolla.

At first, he worked as a dancer and had small parts in movies. Then, in 1921, he became a star in a film called *The Four Horsemen of the Apocalypse*. He followed that success with other hit movies, including *The Sheik* and *Blood and Sand*.

Valentino died at the height of his success, after an ulcer ruptured. Some fans were so upset that they committed suicide. Enormous crowds of adoring women paid their respects at his funeral.

CORNELIUS VANDERBILT
MILLIONAIRE
1794-1877

Starting off with just a rowboat, Cornelius Vanderbilt built a transportation empire that would be worth $96 billion in today's money. As a 16-year-old, Vanderbilt rowed passengers and cargo from Manhattan to Staten Island in New York. By 1829, he had started a steamship company. Less than 20 years later, he had earned his first million.

Vanderbilt was often called "the Commodore" because of his shipping interests. A ruthless businessman, he gave almost none of his vast fortune to charity. One of the few exceptions came late in his life: He gave $1 million to a school in Nashville, Tennessee, which later became Vanderbilt University.

Vincent van Gogh
Artist
1853-1890

In his brief lifetime, Vincent van Gogh *(van GOH)* created 800 oil paintings and 700 drawings. During his life, he sold only one painting, and when he died, few people knew his name. In the years since, however, van Gogh has become world-famous and his work has had a huge influence on modern art.

Van Gogh turned to painting in 1880, after he had a religious crisis. He was largely self-taught. His promising career was cut short by mental illness. Van Gogh decided to kill himself rather than lose control of his mind. Today, he is considered the greatest Dutch artist, after Rembrandt. The paintings of this once-penniless artist now sell for many millions of dollars each.

Amerigo Vespucci
Explorer
1454-1512

Ever wonder where the name *America* comes from? The continents of North America and South America are named after Amerigo Vespucci *(ahm-uh-REE-goh veh-SPOO-chee)*, an Italian explorer.

In 1502, Vespucci wrote a letter claiming to have led four expeditions that explored the New World. At that time, few people in Europe knew that the New World had already been discovered by Christopher Columbus. As a result, one writer gave Vespucci credit, and suggested that the land be given the name *America*.

As it turns out, Vespucci had stretched the truth. He never *led* any expeditions to the Americas—although he may have accompanied three expeditions.

Queen Victoria
Queen of Great Britain
1819-1901

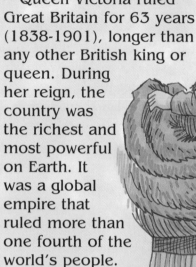

Queen Victoria ruled Great Britain for 63 years (1838-1901), longer than any other British king or queen. During her reign, the country was the richest and most powerful on Earth. It was a global empire that ruled more than one fourth of the world's people.

During Victoria's time on the throne, the role of the British monarch shifted from one of great political power to a mainly ceremonal position. Even so, Victoria was a widely respected queen. Because Great Britain was so powerful, and because Victoria was so well-liked, the late 1800s are often called the Victorian Age.

Virgil
Poet
70-19 B.C.

Virgil is considered the greatest poet of ancient Rome. His most famous work is a lengthy poem called the *Aeneid (ih-NEE-id)*. The *Aeneid* begins where Homer's epic Greek poems, the *Iliad* and the *Odyssey*, left off. It tells the story of a Trojan hero named Aeneas *(ih-NEE-us)*, who escapes from Troy's destruction by the Greeks. He then goes on to found a city that eventually becomes Rome.

Virgil died before he could finish the *Aeneid*. He asked his friends to destroy it because he didn't think it was good enough. However, they saved it, and it became one of the most important long poems in history.

Voltaire
Philosopher
1694-1778

In the 1700s, France was ruled by two groups: royal families and the Roman Catholic Church. Voltaire *(vole-TAIR)* used his witty sense of humor to attack both. As a result, he became one of the best-known playwrights and philosophers in the world. *Voltaire* was the pen name of François Marie Arouet. He was a leader of the Enlightenment, a period when Europeans questioned old political and religious ideas.

Voltaire's writings greatly angered powerful people, and his work was often banned. For instance, although Voltaire believed in God, he was critical of organized religion. His best-known work today is a witty, philosophical novel called *Candide*, which has been adapted into musicals and plays.

Lech Walesa
Labor Leader and President of Poland
1943-

In the early 1980s, Polish workers were unhappy with their country's communist government. They faced high prices and poor working conditions, and were allowed little freedom. Many of them organized into unions, and Lech Walesa *(lek vah-WEN-sah)* became their leader. Walesa, a shipyard electrician, eventually became head of a group called Solidarity, which spoke for all the Polish unions.

Walesa was harassed by Poland's government in an attempt to keep him in line. However, his efforts won Solidarity worldwide attention and support. In 1983, he was awarded the Nobel Peace Prize. His work helped cause communism to fall in Poland and other Eastern European countries in 1989. Walesa was elected president of Poland in 1990 and served until 1995.

MADAME C. J. WALKER
ENTREPRENEUR
1876-1919

Madame C. J. Walker started life with many strikes against her. She was orphaned at age six. She married at age 14 and had a child, but her husband died when she was 20. Working as a washerwoman, she put herself through night school.

In 1905, Walker invented a method of straightening the tightly curled hair that most African Americans are born with. Her method grew very popular, and she branched out into cosmetics.

Walker's real name was Sarah Breedlove Walker. She became an extremely rare person for her time: a black woman who was also a self-made millionaire.

Andy Warhol
Artist
1930-1987

"Pop" art is a school of art that criticizes the advertising and mass-produced products in American society. During the 1960s, Andy Warhol became the best-known of the pop artists. He painted replicas of Campbell's soup cans and colorful portraits of celebrities, such as movie star Marilyn Monroe.

Warhol, whose real name was Andrew Warhola, began his career as an artist who illustrated ads. Once his art became popular, he made several offbeat movies and was a mainstay on the New York art and cultural scenes. Warhol is also known for declaring that, "In the future, everybody will be world-famous for 15 minutes."

Booker T. Washington
Educator
1856-1915

In 1881, a former slave named Booker T. Washington founded the Tuskegee Normal and Industrial Institute in Tuskegee, Alabama. The school for African Americans held its first classes in an abandoned church and a shack. By 1915, it had 1,500 students, 100 buildings, and a fund of $2 million. Today, it is Tuskegee University.

Washington's success at Tuskegee made him a national celebrity. He believed that blacks should abandon calls for immediate equal rights. Instead, he believed, hard work and thrift would in time win respect among whites. Other black leaders, such as W. E. B. Du Bois (doo BOYS) strongly disagreed with Washington's approach.

George Washington
First U.S. President and Father of His Country
1732-1799

Without George Washington, there probably would be no United States of America. During the American Revolution (1775-1783), he held the ragged Colonial army together and led it to victory against long odds. After the war, many people wanted to make Washington a king. He refused that role, but used his influence to help shape the Constitution that made the U.S. a republic.

In 1788, Washington was elected to be the country's first president. After serving for two terms, he left office and retired to his estate in Mount Vernon, Virginia. Washington remains the most honored person in American history.

MUDDY WATERS
BLUES MUSICIAN
1915-1983

Muddy Waters was the stage name of McKinley Morganfield, one of the all-time great blues guitar players. He grew up picking cotton in Mississippi. As a youth, he taught himself to play the harmonica. By 17, he could play the guitar as well, and soon developed a distinctive style of playing and singing. In 1941, a folklore specialist from the Library of Congress recorded Waters' music to preserve it for scholars.

Waters decided to head north to Chicago to make a living as a musician. He switched to the electric guitar, creating a new style of electric blues. In 1950, he had his first national success with the song "Rolling Stone." Over the next three decades, his music had a huge influence on both rock 'n' roll and the blues.

Maurice Wilkins
1916-

Francis
Crick
1916-

Unravelers of the Mystery of DNA

DNA is a scientific term that stands for *deoxyribonucleic acid*. It is the substance that makes up the genes of all living things. It decides whether we have eyes that are blue or brown, hair that is blond or black.

In 1953, biologists James Watson and Francis Crick figured out that DNA has a structure shaped like a *double helix*—kind of like a twisting staircase. Their model showed how genes can duplicate themselves, answering one of biology's most important questions.

Watson's and Crick's discovery was made possible by the work of scientist Maurice Wilkins. In 1962, the three men shared the Nobel Prize for medicine.

James Watson
1928-

James Watt
Inventor Who Made Steam Power Useful
1736-1819

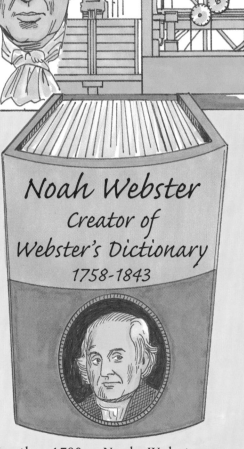

Scottish inventor James Watt did not invent the steam enginer, but he did make it practical. In 1769, he discovered a way to make steam engines use their power more efficiently. Before Watt, steam engines had only limited uses in industry. Because of his improvements, the steam engine helped fuel the Industrial Revolution in England. During that period—from about 1760 to 1860—factories replaced farms as the most important source of income. Living standards improved greatly.

Watt made other advances in the steam engine, and became rich. The units of power called *watts* were named in his honor.

Noah Webster
Creator of Webster's Dictionary
1758-1843

ORSON WELLES
MOVIE ACTOR AND DIRECTOR
1915-1985

In the 1780s, Noah Webster was a schoolteacher in Goshen, New York. He compiled his first dictionary for students. It quickly became a best-seller.

In 1807, Webster began work on his *American Dictionary of the English Language*. The book took 10 years of careful research. It included 12,000 words and at least 30,000 definitions that had never been included in any other dictionary. Published in 1828, Webster's book soon became the standard American dictionary. Revised many times since, it has remained a great influence on the spelling and pronunciation of American English.

On October 30, 1938, Orson Welles accidentally played what may be the biggest practical joke of all time. He directed a radio play based on *The War of the Worlds*, an H. G. Wells novel about a Martian invasion of Earth. The broadcast of the play, done in the style of news bulletins, was so convincing that thousands of Americans panicked. They thought that real Martians were invading.

Welles next went to Hollywood. In 1941, he made *Citizen Kane*, a movie based on the life of William Randolph Hearst, a newspaper millionaire. *Citizen Kane* was a box-office flop at the time, but it is now considered one of the greatest Hollywood films ever made. In 1970, Welles was given a special Academy Award for his pioneering work.

IDA B. WELLS-BARNETT
JOURNALIST AND CIVIL-RIGHTS CRUSADER
1862–1931

A *lynching* is when a mob takes the law into its own hands and kills someone it thinks is guilty of a crime or other offense—whether that person actually is or not. Lynch mobs usually kill by hanging their victims. Between 1882 and 1968, about 4,752 Americans were lynched. Most of those lynch victims—3,445 of them—were black.

Lynching peaked in the U.S. in 1892, with 230 deaths. Three of the people killed that year were friends of Ida B. Wells-Barnett, an African American journalist. The murders prompted her to investigate lynchings and other attacks on black Americans. She braved threats to her own life to keep writing and speaking out about that cruel practice.

Wells-Barnett's work raised awareness about lynchings, and several antilynching groups formed to combat it. She also worked hard to win the right to vote for women.

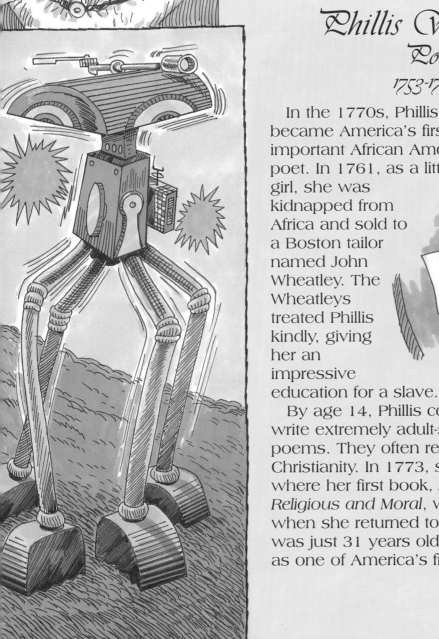

Phillis Wheatley
Poet
1753-1784

In the 1770s, Phillis Wheatley became America's first important African American poet. In 1761, as a little girl, she was kidnapped from Africa and sold to a Boston tailor named John Wheatley. The Wheatleys treated Phillis kindly, giving her an impressive education for a slave.

By age 14, Phillis could write extremely adult-sounding poems. They often reflected her faith in Christianity. In 1773, she went to London, where her first book, *Poems on Various Subjects Religious and Moral*, was published. Phillis was freed when she returned to Boston. She died when she was just 31 years old, but she is recognized today as one of America's first African American poets.

Eli Whitney
Inventor of the Cotton Gin
1765-1825

In the 1700s, cotton farmers in the South had a problem. It was difficult to separate the cotton seeds from the cotton fiber. Whitney solved their problem in 1793 by inventing the cotton gin. It could clean cotton quickly. Cotton production quickly soared from 3,000 bales per year to 73,000 bales per year.

Whitney's invention had an unintended side effect. Before the cotton gin came along, slavery was dying out in the South. However, the jump in cotton production made cheap slave labor more valuable than ever to cotton farmers.

Whitney later promoted the use of interchangeable parts in machines. That idea led to the creation of more mass-produced goods.

Laura Ingalls Wilder
Children's Author
1867-1957

When Laura Ingalls was a girl, her family moved around in frontier areas in Minnesota, Iowa, and the Dakota Territory. Life was hard: The Ingalls family endured disease, conflicts with Indians, and poor harvests.

In 1885, Ingalls married Almanzo Wilder and continued the hard life of farming. Not until she was in her 60s did she take her daughter's advice and begin writing about her childhood.

The results were such books as *Little House in the Big Woods* and *Little House on the Prairie*. These warm, accurate stories became instant classics. They later inspired a television series (1974-1983) called *Little House on the Prairie*.

Thornton Wilder
Novelist and Playwright
1897-1975

In 1928, Thornton Wilder's novel *The Bridge of San Luis Rey* won him the Pulitzer Prize and catapulted him to national fame. That book, which tells the story of five people who were killed when a bridge collapsed in Peru, remains a favorite with readers.

Wilder also won Pulitzer Prizes for two plays, *Our Town* (1938) and *The Skin of Our Teeth* (1942). *Our Town* tells a warm-hearted story about life and death in a small New England town, while *The Skin of Our Teeth* celebrates the human ability to survive almost anything. Another play by Wilder, *The Matchmaker*, was later adapted into a hit musical play and film called *Hello, Dolly!*

Ted Williams
Slugging Star
1918-

In 1941, Boston Red Sox outfielder Ted Williams racked up a season batting average of .406. No professional baseball player has been able to match that accomplishment since. Williams played from 1939 to 1960 and ended his career with a .344 average and 521 home runs.

During World War II (1939-1945) and the Korean War (1950-1953), Williams served as a pilot in the Marine Corps. That forced him to miss five baseball seasons and probably hurt his career statistics. Even so, he is considered one of the greatest hitters ever. In 1966, Williams was elected to the National Baseball Hall of Fame.

WOW! WHAT A HITTER!

Tennessee Williams
Playwright
1911-1983

Tennessee Williams was perhaps the most famous American playwright of the 1950s. Two of his plays—*A Streetcar Named Desire* and *Cat on a Hot Tin Roof*—won Pulitzer Prizes. Another play, *The Glass Menagerie*, is counted among his finest works.

Although he used the pen name Tennessee, Thomas Lanier Williams was born in Columbus, Mississippi. Most of his plays were set in the South. They often showed the tragic destruction of sensitive people by a coarse, unfeeling society. After 1960, Williams's ability to write was hurt by his poor health and addiction to drugs and alcohol. The plays he wrote during the 1950s, however, are considered classics. They are still staged regularly, and several have been made into films.

Woodrow Wilson
28th U.S. President
1856-1924

Woodrow Wilson was president of the United States from 1913 to 1921. He struggled to keep the U.S. out of World War I, which broke out in Europe in 1914. However, German submarine attacks on U.S. ships provoked the U.S. into joining the war in 1917. U.S. troops helped defeat Germany the following year.

Wilson offered generous peace terms to Germany and tried to set up a League of Nations—an early version of the United Nations (UN). That work won him the 1919 Nobel Peace Prize. The League failed, however, because Britain and France, which were U.S. allies, demanded that Germany be punished for its part in the war. Also, Wilson could not convince Congress to allow the U.S. join the League. Wilson's health failed soon after, and he died a bitter man. He is still considered one of the most visionary U.S. presidents.

Oprah Winfrey
Talk-show Host and Actor
1954-

Oprah Winfrey is a powerful force in the entertainment business. In 1984, she launched a daytime talk show now known as *The Oprah Winfrey Show*. Her open, honest style made it a ratings leader for many years. The show also made Winfrey a millionaire.

In 1997, Winfrey began an on-air book club. Books chosen by the club became best-sellers, giving Winfrey enormous clout in the publishing world. In 2000, she launched *O: The Oprah Magazine*. Winfrey, who is also an actor, has appeared in several movies. She earned an Academy Award nomination for her role in *The Color Purple*.

Victoria Woodhull
Women's-rights Activist
1838-1927

I WISH I COULD'VE DONE WHAT OPRAH DOES!

In 1872, Victoria Woodhull became the first woman to run for president of the United States. She ran as the candidate of the Equal Rights Party to protest the fact that women were not allowed to vote.

Woodhull learned to live by her wits at an early age. As a teenager, she supported herself by claiming to be a psychic. With help from the millionaire Cornelius Vanderbilt, she set up a successful stock-brokerage firm.

Although Woodhull was an eloquent speaker, she was not accepted by other women's-rights activists. She held many controversial views that shocked the people of her day.

Tiger Woods
Champion Golfer
1975-

In 1997, Tiger Woods became the youngest golfer ever to win the Masters, one of the biggest events in professional golf. Woods, who is of African American and Asian American descent, was also the first person of color to win the Masters. He shot a tournament record 270 over 72 holes and completely dominated the other players. Born Eldrick Woods, he showed a genius for golf as a little boy. At age 15, he became the youngest winner of the U.S. Junior Amateur championship. In 2000, he set a record by winning the U.S. Open golf tournament by a record 15 strokes. In April 2001, Woods won his second Masters. Combined with the titles that he won in 2000, that made him the first-ever golfer to hold all four Grand Slam event titles at the same time. The Grand Slam events—the most important in pro golf—are the Masters, the U.S. Open, the British Open, and the Professional Golfers' Association (PGA) Championship.

I SURE HOPE THIS WON'T HURT!

FRANK LLOYD WRIGHT
ARCHITECT
1867-1959

Frank Lloyd Wright greatly changed architecture during the 20th century. One of his most enduring achievements is the "prairie style" house, designed to blend in with its natural surroundings.

Wright's buildings were solidly built as well as interesting to look at. In 1916, he designed Tokyo's Imperial Hotel to be able to withstand earthquakes. He did it well: In 1923, that city was wiped out by a major quake, but Wright's hotel remained undamaged.

Wright designed other famous buildings, such as the Guggenheim Museum in New York and the Marin County Civic Center in California. Many people have criticized the space-age look of Wright's designs. However, his style has been widely copied.

Wilbur Wright
1867-1912

The First People to Fly

Orville Wright
1871-1948

On December 17, 1903, Orville and Wilbur Wright flew the world's first airplane on the windblown sands of Kitty Hawk, North Carolina. Since the 1700s, people had been able to fly using balloons and gliders.

Before the Wright brothers, however, nobody had ever flown a machine that was heavier than air.

Prior to the Wrights' flight, many people had falsely claimed to have created flying machines. As a result, newspapers ignored the Wrights at first. After all, they were just a pair of bicycle-shop owners from Dayton, Ohio. It took years—and several demonstration flights—for the Wrights to prove that they really had solved the mystery of flight.

William Butler Yeats
Poet
1865-1939

Many people consider William Butler Yeats (*yayts*) to be the finest poet of the 20th century. His poem "The Second Coming" is one of the most quoted works in the English language.

Yeats led the efforts to revive Irish literature in the late 1800s and early 1900s. At that time, Ireland was part of Great Britain. Yeats and other Irish writers shifted the focus of their work from English culture to Irish culture. Yeats also championed Irish independence from Great Britain.

In addition to poems, Yeats wrote 26 plays. He won the 1923 Nobel Prize for literature.

Boris Yeltsin
Former President of Russia
1931-

In 1990, Boris Yeltsin became the first freely elected president of Russia. At that time, Russia was still part of the Soviet Union, and Yeltsin had to answer to Soviet leader Mikhail Gorbachev (*gore-buh-CHAWF*).

That changed in 1991, when conservative communists overthrew Gorbachev. Their takeover lasted two days. It was crushed by democratic forces led by Yeltsin. Soon afterward, the Soviet Union broke up into 15 countries, including Russia.

Yeltsin led Russia through the stormy change from communism to democracy. Despite some successes, the country became swamped by crime and corruption. Yeltsin's health problems and unpopularity forced him to resign in 1999.

Brigham Young
Leader of the Mormon Church
1801-1877

In 1830, Joseph Smith of Fayette, New York, founded the Mormon Church and published the Book of Mormon. His followers, called Mormons, believed that Smith was God's prophet and that the book was divinely inspired.

At first, Mormons faced hostility from many non-Mormons, and Smith was murdered in 1844. Brigham Young, one of his followers, took over control of the church. In 1848, Young led the Mormons to the deserts of Utah and founded Salt Lake City.

Young remained the Mormons' leader, but he was controversial with non-Mormons. Mormons believed in taking many wives, and Young had more than 20. That practice was banned by the church after Young's death.

BECAUSE OF THE WAY HE PITCHED, HE GOT THE NAME OF "CY"—SHORT FOR CYCLONE!

THEY NAMED AN AWARD AFTER THIS GUY!

Cy Young
Pitching Superstar
1867-1955

Right-hander Cy Young won more major-league baseball games than any other pitcher in history. Although many early baseball records are in dispute, Young won at least 509 games. In 16 of the 22 years he played, Young won 20 or more games. In five of those years, he won 30 or more games.

Born Denton True Young, he spent most of his career with the Cleveland Spiders and the Boston Red Sox. In 1937, he was elected to the National Baseball Hall of Fame. At the end of each season, each league—the American and the National—gives a Cy Young Award to its best pitcher.

Babe Didrickson Zaharias
Athlete
1911-1956

FORE!

FOUR?

Mildred Ella Didrickson (*DID-rik-sun*) got her nickname "Babe" as an athletic young girl. She reminded people of Babe Ruth because she hit so many home runs. She went on to become the greatest female athlete of the 20th century.

At the 1932 Olympics, she won two gold medals in track and field. She also was a standout athlete in softball, baseball, swimming, figure skating, and football. Later in the 1930s, she married wrestler George Zaharias and turned her attention to golf. In 1948, she became a pro golfer and dominated the sport until 1954. She also helped found the Ladies Professional Golf Association (LPGA).

EMILIANO ZAPATA
MEXICAN REVOLUTIONARY
1880-1919

Emiliano Zapata (*eh-mee-LYAH-noh sah-PAH-tah*) was an important figure in the Mexican Revolution (1910-1920). He controlled a powerful guerrilla army. At one point, it numbered more than 25,000 men.

Zapata was a champion of the poor. One of his main goals was to take land from wealthy owners and give it to Mexico's starving poor. The terrible fighting and confusion that took place during the revolution made that goal difficult to achieve. However, Zapata won praise from outsiders for his reforms and for the order he maintained.

Like many revolutionary leaders, he was eventually betrayed, ambushed, and killed.

Zhou Enlai
Communist Leader
1898-1976

Zhou Enlai (*JOE en-LYE*) joined the Communist Party as a young man and helped it seize control of China's government in 1949. He became a close associate of communist ruler Mao Zedong (*mow zeh-dong*).

Zhou tried to ease the pain caused by Mao's radical policies. For instance, in the 1960s, Mao launched a campaign against intellectuals called the Cultural Revolution. Zhou protected some of the people who were being attacked during that time.

In 1972, he helped mend U.S.-China relations by arranging a meeting between Mao and U.S. President Richard Nixon. He also helped moderate leaders rise to power in China's government.

Zhang Qian
Explorer
100s B.C.

In 138 B.C., the Chinese emperor Wu Di wanted to make a military alliance with a tribe living in the far west of China. Whoever he sent, though, would have to cross thousands of miles of enemy territory. Zhang Qian volunteered for the job.

Zhang's 100-man party was captured right away and held for 10 years. He escaped to complete his mission, but found that the tribe did not want to help China's emperor.

Instead, after 13 years away, Zhang returned to China with information about faraway people and cities. His journey led to the creation of the Silk Road, a major trade route between the ancient empires of China and Rome.

Shaka Zulu
Dictator and
Military Genius
1787-1828

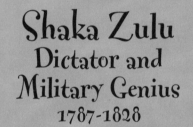

In 1816, Shaka became king of the Zulu tribe in what is now South Africa. He turned the tribe into a fearsome war machine. Shaka gave the tribe improved weapons—a cowhide shield and a short stabbing spear. He also created new fighting tactics. Shaka's goal was always to surround an enemy army and destroy it completely.

Soon, no tribe could withstand a Zulu attack. Shaka controlled a large empire and he ruled with an iron fist. Anyone suspected of opposing him was killed. In 1927, Shaka's mother died and he went insane, killing thousands of Zulus. The next year, Shaka Zulu was assassinated by family members.

Index

Mao Zedong, 107
Medici, Cosimo de', 112
Medici, Giovanni de', 112
Medici, Lorenzo de', 112
Medici, Catherine de', 112
Minamoto Yoritomo, 116
Montezuma II, 117
Mussolini, Benito, 120
Napoleon I, 121
Nefertiti, 121
Peter the Great, 134
Pu Yi, 139
Ramses II, 139
Shih Huangdi, 157
Suleiman I, 163
Tojo, Hideki, 167
Tutankhamen, 169
Victoria, 172
Zulu, Shaka, 185

Saints
Joan of Arc, 88

Scientists
Aristotle, 14
Audubon, John Jacob, 16
Burbank, Luther, 31
Carson, Rachel, 34
Carver, George Washington, 35
Copernicus, Nicolaus, 42
Cousteau, Jacques-Yves, 44
Crick, Francis, 175
Curie, Marie, 45
Darwin, Charles, 47
Einstein, Albert, 57
Fermi, Enrico, 60
Fleming, Alexander, 61
Fossey, Dian, 62
Franklin, Benjamin, 63
Galen, 65
Galileo, 65
Goddard, Robert, 70
Goodall, Jane, 71
Halley, Edmond, 74
Hawking, Stephen, 76
Hubble, Edwin, 83
Kepler, Johannes, 93
Leakey, Louis, 97
Leakey, Mary, 97
Leakey, Richard, 97
Leonardo da Vinci, 48,
Linnaeus, Carolus, 100
Mendel, Gregor, 113
Mendeleev, Dmitri, 114
Muir, John, 120
Newton, Isaac, 122
Nobel, Alfred, 124
Oppenheimer, J. Robert, 127
Pascal, Blaise, 130
Pasteur, Louis, 131
Pavlov, Ivan, 132
Sabin, Albert, 150
Sagan, Carl, 151
Salk, Jonas, 150
Watson, James, 175

Wilkins, Maurice, 175
Women's-rights Activists
Anthony, Susan B., 12
Friedan, Betty, 63
Stanton, Elizabeth Cady, 161
Stone, Lucy, 162
Woodhull, Victoria, 180
World Travelers, *see also*
     EXPLORERS
da Gama, Vasco, 46
Ibn Battuta, 21
Polo, Marco, 137
Writers, *see also* HISTORIANS
Aeschylus, 9
Aesop, 10
Alcott, Louisa May, 10
Andersen, Hans Christian, 11
Asimov, Isaac, 15
Austen, Jane, 17
Baldwin, James, 18
Beckett, Samuel, 22
Blume, Judy, 26
Brecht, Bertolt, 29
Brontë, Anne, 29
Brontë, Charlotte, 29
Brontë, Emily, 29
Carroll, Lewis, 33
Cervantes, Miguel de, 36
Chaucer, Geoffrey, 38
Chekkov, Anton, 38
Dickens, Charles, 51
Dickinson, Emily, 51
Dostoevsky, Fyodor, 52
Doyle, Arthur Conan, 53
Ellison, Ralph, 58
Euripides, 59
Frank, Anne, 62
Frost, Robert, 64
Grimm, Jakob, 73
Grimm, Wilhelm, 73
Hemingway, Ernest, 77
Homer, 81
Hughes, Langston, 82
Ibsen, Henrik, 84
Irving, Washington, 85
Kerouac, Jack, 93
Key, Francis Scott, 94
Lewis, Sinclair, 99
London, Jack, 102
Melville, Herman, 113
Millay, Edna St. Vincent, 115
Miller, Arthur, 115
Milne, Alan Alexander, 115
Mitchell, Margaret, 116
Morrison, Toni, 118
Mother Goose, 19
Nostradamus, 125
O'Neill, Eugene, 126
Orwell, George, 127
Poe, Edgar Allan, 136
Potter, Beatrix, 137
Sendak, Maurice, 153
Seneca the Younger, 154

Seuss, Dr.,155
Shakespeare, William, 155
Shaw, George Bernard, 156
Shelley, Mary, 156
Sophocles, 158
Stevenson, Robert Louis, 161
Stowe, Harriet Beecher, 162
Thoreau, Henry David, 166
Tolstoy, Leo, 167
Twain, Mark, 170
Virgil, 172
Wheatley, Phillis, 177
Wilder, Laura Ingalls, 178
Wilder, Thornton, 178
Williams, Tennessee, 179
Yeats, William Butler, 182

Hank Aaron

The Beatles

Mary Cassatt

Galileo

Hirohito

Washington Irving

Madonna

Nefertiti

Annie Oakley

Shirley Temple

Vincent van Gogh

Andy Warhol